A NavPress Bible study on the book of

# ACTS

NAVPRESS

A MINISTRY OF THE NAVIGATORS
P.O. BOX 35001, COLORADO SPRINGS, COLORADO 80935

The Navigators is an international Christian organization. Jesus Christ gave His followers the Great Commission to go and make disciples (Matthew 28:19). The aim of The Navigators is to help fulfill that commission by multiplying laborers for Christ in every nation.

NavPress is the publishing ministry of The Navigators. NavPress publications are tools to help Christians grow. Although publications alone cannot make disciples or change lives, they can help believers learn biblical discipleship, and apply what they learn to their lives and ministries.


ISBN 08910-91122

Seventh printing, 1993



Printed in the United States of America

---



---

# CONTENTS

# ACKNOWLEDGMENTS

This LIFECHANGE study has been produced through the coordinated efforts of a team of Navigator Bible study developers and NavPress editorial staff, along with a nationwide network of fieldtesters.

*SERIES EDITOR: KAREN HINCKLEY*

# HOW TO USE THIS STUDY

## Objectives

Each guide in the LIFECHANGE series of Bible studies covers one book of the Bible. Although the LIFECHANGE guides vary with the individual books they explore, they share some common goals:

1. To provide you with a firm foundation of understanding and a thirst to return to the book;
2. To teach you by example how to study a book of the Bible without structured guides;
3. To give you all the historical background, word definitions, and explanatory notes you need, so that your only other reference is the Bible;
4. To help you grasp the message of the book as a whole;
5. To teach you how to let God's Word transform you into Christ's image.

Each lesson in this study is designed to take 60 to 90 minutes to complete on your own. The guide is based on the assumption that you are completing one lesson per week, but if time is limited you can do half a lesson per week or whatever amount allows you to be thorough.

## Flexibility

LIFECHANGE guides are flexible, allowing you to adjust the quantity and depth of your study to meet your individual needs. The guide offers many optional questions in addition to the regular numbered questions. The optional questions, which appear in the margins of the study pages, include the following:

*Optional Application.* Nearly all application questions are optional; we hope you will do as many as you can without overcommitting yourself.

*For Thought and Discussion.* Beginning Bible students should be able to handle these, but even advanced students need to think about them. These questions frequently deal with ethical issues and other biblical principles. They often offer cross-references to spark thought, but the references do not give obvious answers. They are good for group discussions.

*For Further Study*. These include: a) cross-references that shed light on a topic the book discusses, and b) questions that delve deeper into the passage. You can omit them to shorten a lesson without missing a major point of the passage.

(Note: At the end of lessons two through nineteen you are given the option of outlining the passage just studied. Although the outline is optional, you will probably find it worthwhile.)

If you are meeting in a group, decide together which optional questions to prepare for each lesson, and how much of the lesson you will cover at the next meeting. Normally, the group leader should make this decision, but you might let each member choose his or her own application questions.

As you grow in your walk with God, you will find the LIFECHANGE guide growing with you—a helpful reference on a topic, a continuing challenge for application, a source of questions for many levels of growth.

## Overview and Details

The guide begins with an overview of the book. The key to interpretation is context—what is the whole passage or book *about*?—and the key to context is purpose—what is the author's *aim* for the whole work? In lesson one you will lay the foundation for your study by asking yourself, Why did the author (and God) write the book? What did they want to accomplish? What is the book about?

Then, in lesson two, you will begin analyzing successive passages in detail. Thinking about how a paragraph fits into the overall goal of the book will help you to see its purpose. Its purpose will help you see its meaning. Frequently reviewing a chart or outline of the book will enable you to make these connections.

Finally, in the last lesson, you will review the whole book, returning to the big picture to see whether your view of it has changed after closer study. Review will also strengthen your grasp of major issues and give you an idea of how you have grown from your study.

## Kinds of Questions

Bible study on your own—without a structured guide—follows a progression. First you observe: What does the passage *say*? Then you interpret: What does the passage *mean*? Lastly you apply: How does this truth affect my life?

Some of the "how" and "why" questions will take some creative thinking, even prayer, to answer. Some are opinion questions without clearcut right answers; these will lend themselves to discussions and side studies.

Don't let your study become an exercise of knowledge alone. Treat the passage as God's Word, and stay in dialogue with Him as you study. Pray, "Lord, what do You want me to see here?" "Father, why is this true?" "Lord, how does this apply to my life?"

It is important that you write down your answers. The act of writing clarifies your thinking and helps you to remember.

Meditating on verses is an option in several lessons. Its purpose is to let biblical truth sink into your inner convictions so that you will increasingly be able to act on this truth as a natural way of life. You may want to find a quiet place to spend five minutes each day repeating the verse(s) to yourself. Think about what each word, phrase, and sentence means to you. At intervals throughout the rest of the day, remind yourself of the verse(s).

## Study Aids

A list of reference materials, including a few notes of explanation to help you make good use of them, begins on page 213. This guide is designed to include enough background to let you interpret with just your Bible and the guide. Still, if you want more information on a subject or want to study a book on your own, try the references listed.

## Scripture Versions

Unless otherwise indicated, the Bible quotations in this guide are from the New International Version of the Bible. Other versions cited are the Revised Standard Version (RSV), the New American Standard Bible (NASB), and the King James Version (KJV).

Use any translation you like for study, preferably more than one. A paraphrase such as The Living Bible is not accurate enough for study, but it can be helpful for comparison or devotional reading.

## Memorizing and Meditating

A Psalmist wrote, "I have hidden your word in my heart that I might not sin against you" (Psalm 119:11). If you write down a verse or passage that challenges or encourages you, and reflect on it often for a week or more, you will find it beginning to affect your motives and actions. We forget quickly what we read once; we remember what we ponder.

When you find a significant verse or passage, you might copy it onto a card to keep with you. Set aside five minutes during each day just to think about what the passage might mean in your life. Recite it over to yourself, exploring its meaning. Then, return to your passage as often as you can during your day, for a brief review. You will soon find it coming to mind spontaneously.

## For Group Study

A group of four to ten people allows the richest discussions, but you can adapt this guide for other sized groups. It will suit a wide range of group types, such as home Bible studies, growth groups, youth groups, and businessmen's studies.

Both new and experienced Bible students, and new and mature Christians, will benefit from the guide. You can omit or leave for later years any questions you find too easy or too hard.

The guide is intended to lead a group through one lesson per week. However, feel free to split lessons if you want to discuss them more thoroughly. Or, omit some questions in a lesson if preparation or discussion time is limited. You can always return to this guide for personal study later. You will be able to discuss only a few questions at length, so choose some for discussion and others for background. Make time at each discussion for members to ask about anything they didn't understand.

Each lesson in the guide ends with a section called "For the group." These sections give advice on how to focus a discussion, how you might apply the lesson in your group, how you might shorten a lesson, and so on. The group leader should read each "For the group" at least a week ahead so that he or she can tell the group how to prepare for the next lesson.

Each member should prepare for a meeting by writing answers for all the background and discussion questions to be covered. If the group decides not to take an hour per week for private preparation, then expect to take at least two meetings per lesson to work through the questions. Application will be very difficult, however, without private thought and prayer.

Two reasons for studying in a group are accountability and support. When each member commits in front of the rest to seek growth in an area of life, you can pray with one another, listen jointly for God's guidance, help one another to resist temptation, assure each other that the other's growth matters to you, use the group to practice spiritual principles, and so on. Pray about one another's commitments and needs at most meetings. Spend the first few minutes of each meeting sharing any results from applications prompted by previous lessons. Then discuss new applications toward the end of the meeting. Follow such sharing with prayer for these and other needs.

If you write down each other's applications and prayer requests, you are more likely to remember to pray for them during the week, ask about them at the next meeting, and notice answered prayers. You might want to get a notebook for prayer requests and discussion notes.

Notes taken during discussion will help you to remember, follow up on ideas, stay on the subject, and clarify a total view of an issue. But don't let note-taking keep you from participating. Some groups choose one member at each meeting to take notes. Then someone copies the notes and distributes them at the next meeting. Rotating these tasks can help include people. Some groups have someone take notes on a large pad of paper or erasable marker board (preformed shower wallboard works well), so that everyone can see what has been recorded.

Pages 215-216 list some good sources of counsel for leading group studies. *The Small Group Letter,* published by NavPress, is unique, offering insights from experienced leaders every other month.

LESSON ONE

# OVERVIEW

## What Is Acts?

The Holy Spirit has given us in the New Testament four accounts of Jesus' ministry but only one book on the early years of the Church. It is called the Acts of the Apostles, but in fact it tells us only selected things about a few of the apostles. What about John, who gave us five of the New Testament books? What about Matthew, who wrote one Gospel? What about Andrew, Thomas, Bartholemew, James the Younger, Simon the Zealot, Judas son of James, and Matthias? Acts is even silent on the last fifteen years or so of Peter's ministry. Clearly, just as God has not chosen to give us a complete biography of Jesus, so He has determined not to inspire a thorough history of the Church's beginnings.[1]

### What is Acts?

If Acts is not a complete history of the Church's first three decades, then what is it? Our first clue is that it is the second of a two-volume work. An early convert to Christianity named Luke wrote a Gospel and Acts for a Roman aristocrat named Theophilus (Luke 1:1-4, Acts 1:1). Luke was the "beloved physician" (Colossians 4:14, NASB) of the Apostle Paul. He traveled with Paul on part of his second missionary journey. Some years later, Luke went from Philippi to Jerusalem with Paul, and when Paul was arrested there, Luke accompanied him on his harrowing journey to Rome. We surmise these facts from the way Luke changed from the third person ("they") to the first ("we") in parts of Acts (16:10-17, 20:5-21:18, 27:1-28:16).

We don't know whether Luke was a Gentile, a Gentile convert to Judaism, or a Jew before he became a Christian. His writings show that he was steeped in the urban, Gentile, Greek-speaking culture of the Roman Empire; Luke 1:1-4 is written in the literary Greek of the educated elite, and Acts describes Gentile kings, philosophers, and legal details accurately. On the other hand, Luke was also well versed in the *Septuagint*, the Greek translation of the Old Testament that Jews all over the Empire used.

About Theophilus we can only speculate. His name means "lover of God," but it was a common Greek name and was probably not made up by Luke. In Luke's day, people often wrote for and dedicated their works to wealthy patrons, who helped pay for publishing the books. Theophilus was probably an educated Gentile aristocrat, either a new convert or an interested pagan. Luke may have wanted to help confirm this man and others like him in the faith by showing that it rested on firm historical foundations and the power of God.

When was Acts written? The earliest would be about 62 AD, where chapter 28 leaves off abruptly. However, Luke seems to be looking back on those events from at least some distance. On the other hand, the book gives no hint of the deaths of Paul, Peter, or James, nor of the destruction of Jerusalem in 70 AD, nor even of Paul's letters. Would a book written after 90 AD partly about Paul have ignored his letters, which were so influential by then? Most scholars who think Acts is an accurate account by Luke (as opposed to fiction) guess that the book was written over some time and finished "towards AD 70."[2]

1. Look at Luke's prologue to his whole work (Luke 1:1-4). What does he say Luke-Acts is meant to be?

______________________________________________

______________________________________________

______________________________________________

______________________________________________

2. In Acts 1:1-2, Luke summarizes volume 1 (Luke's Gospel) as an introduction to volume 2 (Acts). He says the Gospel is about "all that Jesus began to do and to teach" until His ascension into Heaven forty days after the Resurrection. If Luke's Gospel is about what Jesus *began* to do and to teach, what is Acts probably about?

______________________________________________

______________________________________________

______________________________________________

______________________________________________

3. What does Acts 1:8 tell you about the purpose of the book?

______________________________________________

______________________________________________

______________________________________________

4. Read 1:15, 2:41, 4:4, 5:14, 6:7, 9:31, 12:24, 16:5, 19:20, and 28:31.

a. What do these verses have in common, and what progression do you see?

______________________________

______________________________

______________________________

______________________________

______________________________

______________________________

b. What does this pattern tell you about Acts?

______________________________

______________________________

______________________________

______________________________

______________________________

______________________________

Acts does not tell us *all* that Jesus did through the apostles, but only some of what He did through some of them. We learn nothing about the spread of the gospel to "Crete (Titus 1:5), Illyricum (Romans 15:19—modern Yugoslavia), or Pontus, Cappadocia and Bithynia (1 Peter 1:1), not to mention the church's expansion eastward toward Mesopotamia or southward toward Egypt."[3] Instead, Luke focuses on one line of geographical expansion: from Jerusalem to Rome. Therefore, Acts 1:8 is only a partial clue to the book's theme.

Also, Luke is not concerned to give us the apostles' biographies. He begins with the apostles in Jerusalem, then ignores most of them to focus on Peter and two non-apostles. Then he turns from Peter to Paul, and he ends the book at last with Paul a prisoner in Rome probably destined to live several more years.

Moreover, Luke does not tell us all we might like to know about organization, lifestyle, and worship in the early Church. He gives us glimpses of details, but these are incidental to the focus of the story.

What is the main focus? The best way to find this out (indeed, the best way to begin studying any book) is to read it several times, noting first impressions and the major sections. If possible, you should stop now and read through Acts once. Then, get a piece of paper, go back through the book, and write down what each of the following sections is about:

1:1-6:7
6:8-9:31
9:32-12:24
12:25-16:5
16:6-19:20
19:21-28:31

This whole procedure should take you four to five hours, but Acts is a terrific story so it should be fun. However, if you don't have time for this kind of preparation, you can look at the following outlines before you read the book.

Acts can be outlined in several ways. We can divide chapters 1-12 (which focus on Peter and the Jewish mission) from chapters 13-28 (which focus on Paul and the Gentile mission). Or, we can use 1:8 as a framework, like this:

Jerusalem (1:1-7:60)
Samaria and Judea (8:1-10:48)
The ends of the earth (11:1-28:31)

Thirdly, we can combine these two views, like this:[4]

I. Peter and the Beginnings of the Church in Palestine (chapters 1-12)
  A. "Throughout Judea, Galilee and Samaria" (1:1-9:31; see 9:31)
  B. "As far as Phoenicia, Cyprus and Antioch" (9:32-12:25; see 11:19)
II. Paul and the Expansion of the Church from Antioch to Rome (chapters 13-28)
  A. "Throughout the region of Phrygia and Galatia" (13:1-15:35; see 16:6)
  B. "Over to Macedonia" (15:36-21:16; see 16:9)
  C. "To Rome" (21:17-28:31; see 28:14)

Finally, we can use those "progress reports" you observed in question 4, like this:

(1:1-6:7) *The earliest church in Jerusalem*: Preaching for Jews, common life among Jewish Christians, worship at the Temple and synagogues, opposition from other Jews. Concludes with a resolved disagreement between Greek- and Aramaic-speaking believers.

(6:8-9:31) *The first geographical expansion*: Greek-speaking Jewish Christians ("Hellenists") bring the gospel to Jews, Samaritans (semi-Jews), and a convert to Judaism. The martyrdom of Stephen (a Hellenist) causes the expansion, and the conversion of Paul (a Jew from outside Palestine) partly results from the expansion.

(9:32-12:24) *The first expansion to the Gentiles*: To make this breakthrough, God uses Peter (an Aramaic-speaking Jew, a "Hebrew") rather than the Hellenists. The Hellenists begin evangelizing Gentiles in Antioch.

(12:25-16:5) *The first geographical expansion into the Gentile world*: Paul leads. When the Church decides that Gentile Christians need not live as Jews, the Gentile mission is free to explode. Opposition is still mainly Jewish.

(16:6-19:20) *Paul's westward expansion reaches Europe.* Jews continue to reject the gospel, and Gentiles continue to accept it. However, success with some Gentiles produces opposition from others.

(19:21-28:31) *Paul reaches Rome with the gospel.* Paul suffers many trials patiently while innocent of wrongdoing.[5]

5. If you have not already done so, read the whole book of Acts, at one sitting if possible. It is one of the finest examples of the kind of history written in the ancient world. You will notice that it is not like the history written today; you'll see few dates but a great concern for the reader's enjoyment. The pace is fast, so you'll scarcely notice that the events of chapter 12 occurred some ten to thirteen years after those of chapter two.

   Use the above outlines, the timeline on page 19, and the map on page 20 to guide your reading. If you want to remember any observations or questions, jot them in the space below. In particular, look for repeated words and patterns of events.

6. One main character dominates the whole of Acts. Who is that character, and what are some of his effects? (See, for instance, 1:8; 2:4; 4:8,31; 8:39; 9:31; 13:4; 15:28; 16:6-10; 20:22-24; 21:10-11.)

7. From your observations so far, what seem to be the central themes, messages, or purposes of Acts?

## Your response

**Study Skill—Application**

Second Timothy 3:16-17 tells us that "All Scripture . . . is useful for teaching, rebuking, correcting and training in righteousness, so that the man of God may be thoroughly equipped for every good work." James 1:22 urges us to do what the Word says, not merely hear it. Therefore, the last step of Bible study is asking ourselves, "What difference should this passage make to my life? How should it make me want to think or act?" Application will require time, thought, prayer, and perhaps even discussion with another person.

If you sometimes have trouble finding a truth in a passage that is relevant to you, consider the following five questions:

Is there a *sin* for me to avoid?
Is there a *promise* for me to trust?
Is there an *example* for me to follow?
Is there a *command* for me to obey?
How can this passage increase my *knowledge* of the Lord (not just knowledge about Him)?

*(continued on page 15)*

*(continued from page 14)*

You can recall these five questions by remembering the acronym SPECK—Sin, Promise, Example, Command, Knowledge.

Look for something specific you can do or pray about in response to the truth (the sin, promise, etc.) that is relevant to you. Ask the Holy Spirit to guide you in choosing and empower you in fulfilling your application. If your application is a change of attitude rather than an action, plan to pray about it daily for awhile, and ask God to show you circumstances in which you can act on your change of attitude.

8. The book of Acts is largely about how the Church fulfilled its mission during its first thirty years (from Jesus' ascension to about 62 AD). Why is it important for us to study this story? How is it relevant to us?

9. a. Did you notice anything in your first reading of Acts that you want to remember and apply? If so, what is the truth you want to take to heart?

   b. Ask God to show you how you can apply this truth, and write your thoughts and plans here.

## For the group

This "For the group" section and the ones in later lessons are intended to suggest ways of structuring your discussions. Feel free to select what suits your group.

The main goals of an introductory lesson are to get to know Acts in general and the people with whom you are going to study it. The group will benefit from having time to read the "How to Use This Study" section on pages 5-8, the whole book of Acts, and the background in this lesson before diving into detailed study.

Later lessons will give more background as necessary on Luke, Jerusalem, the Roman Empire, etc. You might make a list of group members' questions and decide if they need to be answered right away. If so, pages 213-216 list some sources of information. If not, watch for answers later in the study guide.

Some people may not be able to read all of Acts at one time. Encourage everyone to get through it at some point, even if some people need several sittings. (You can plan two meetings for this overview lesson—see suggestions under "Warm-up" below.)

**Worship.** Some groups like to begin meetings with prayer and/or singing. Some prefer to share requests for prayer at the beginning, but leave the actual prayer until after the study. Others prefer just to chat and have refreshments and then move to the study, leaving worship until the end. It is generally good to begin with at least a brief prayer for God's guidance in the study.

**Warm-up.** The beginning of a new study is a good time to lay a foundation for honest sharing of ideas, for getting comfortable with each other, and for encouraging a sense of common purpose. One way to establish common ground is to talk about what each group member hopes to get out of your group—out of your study of Acts, and out of any prayer, singing, sharing, outreach, or anything else you might do together. You can include what you hope to give the group as well. Why are you studying the Bible, and Acts in particular? If you have someone write down each member's hopes and expectations, then you can look back at these goals later to see if they are being met. You can then make changes in your meetings if necessary, such as planning more time for prayer or deciding to cover Acts more slowly.

You can take about fifteen minutes before discussing lesson one to discuss these goals. Or, you can take a whole meeting to introduce the study, discuss the "How to Use This Study" section on pages 5-8, and share your goals. In a second meeting, you can discuss questions 1-9. Doing this will allow the group more time to read Acts and complete lesson one.

**Overview.** You can structure your discussion like this:

1. *How to Use This Study.* The group should have read this section at home. The leader can remind everyone of the main points and ask if anyone has questions about what to do. For example, point out the optional questions

in the margins. These are available as group discussion questions, ideas for application, and suggestions for further study. It is unlikely that anyone will have either the time or desire to answer all the optional questions and do all the applications. It is reasonable to expect a person to do *one* "Optional Application" for any given lesson. You might choose *two* "For Thought and Discussions" for your group discussion. If someone wants to write answers to the optional questions, suggest that he use a separate notebook. It will also be helpful for discussion notes, prayer requests, answers to prayer, application plans, and so on.

Note the observation-interpretation-application pattern in each lesson. Many of the numbered questions are observations and basic interpretations that lay the groundwork for deeper study. The meaty questions are sometimes in the margins. In your group discussion, you may prefer to move quickly through the observation questions in order to concentrate on questions that interest you. Or, you may want to spend more time learning to observe details and leave deeper questions for future years.

Point out the study aids on pages 213-216. If you own any, bring them in to show the group.

2. *First Impressions.* Ask questions to draw out the group's impressions of Acts after one reading. Some possibilities are: "What is Acts about? What are your first impressions of the book? Who are some of the important characters? Tell something about each of those people. Did you enjoy reading the book? Why or why not? What kinds of things happen over and over in the book? What aspects of early Church history do and don't seem to have interested Luke? What did you learn about Luke, the Gospel he wrote, and Acts from the background in lesson one?"

   If you let several people answer questions like these, you should put together a good picture of the book. Then, let some people answer questions 1-7.
3. *Questions.* Don't forget to keep a list of the group's questions as you discuss. You can try to answer them as you go through later lessons.
4. *Application.* If your group is not already familiar with how to apply Scripture to your lives, think of some sample ways you could apply something in Acts. Use the Study Skill on pages 14-15. If the group already understands how to apply, give everyone a chance to share one truth that he or she would like to put into practice this week.

**Wrap-up.** This is a time to bring the discussion to a focused end and to make any announcements about the next lesson or meeting.

Some people tend to prepare for group discussions only one or two days before the meetings and then feel that it is too late to start an application. Tell the group that it is fine to be applying an insight from the previous lesson during the week when you are preparing the next lesson for discussion.

**Worship.** Thank God for the book of Acts and the people described in it. Praise Him for some particular things He has revealed to you about Himself through this book. Ask Him to enable you each to understand and apply what He says to you through Acts.

1. Other books called the Acts of John, the Acts of Peter and Paul, the Acts of Thomas, etc. were written during the Church's first two centuries, but the Church as a whole judged these to be largely fictional and not inspired by God.
2. F. F. Bruce, "The Acts of the Apostles," *The New Bible Commentary: Revised,* edited by Donald Guthrie, et al. (London: Inter-Varsity Press, 1970), pages 968-969; I. Howard Marshall, *The Acts of the Apostles* (Grand Rapids, Michigan: William B. Eerdmans Publishing Company, 1980), pages 46-48.
3. Gordon D. Fee and Douglas Stuart, *How to Read the Bible for All Its Worth* (Grand Rapids, Michigan: Zondervan Corporation, 1982), page 92.
4. Adapted from the outline of Acts by Lewis Foster in *The NIV Study Bible,* edited by Kenneth Barker (Grand Rapids, Michigan: Zondervan Corporation, 1984), page 1643.
5. Adapted from the outline in Fee and Stuart, pages 90-91.

## Ti[illegible]

(A[illegible] F.F. Bruce, *Paul: Apostle of the Heart Set Free,* page 475.)

| | |
|---|---|
| [illegible]urrection; Pentecost | 30 AD |
| [illegible] (Acts 6:8-8:1) | 33 |
| [illegible] (Acts 9:1-19) | 33 |
| [illegible]lem to see Peter (Galatians 1:18) | 35 |
| Paul in [illegible] and Syria (Galatians 1:21, Acts 9:30) | 35-46 |
| Herod Agrippa I dies (Acts 12:19-23) | 44 |
| Paul visits Jerusalem to clarify the mission to the Gentiles (Galatians 2:1-10) | 46 |
| Paul and Barnabas in Cyprus and Galatia (Acts 13-14) | 47-48 |
| Council of Jerusalem (Acts 15) | 49 |
| Paul and Silas travel from Antioch to Asia Minor, Macedonia, and Achaia (Acts 16-17) | 49-50 |
| Paul in Corinth (Acts 18:1-18) | 50-52 |
| Paul visits Jerusalem | 52 |
| Paul in Ephesus (Acts 19) | 52-55 |
| Paul travels to Macedonia, Dalmatia, and Achaia (Acts 20) | 55-57 |
| Paul to Jerusalem (Acts 21:1-23:22) | May 57 |
| Paul imprisoned in Caesarea (Acts 23:23-26:32) | 57-59 |
| Paul sent to house arrest in Rome (Acts 27:1-28:31) | 59-62 |

# Map of the Roman Empire

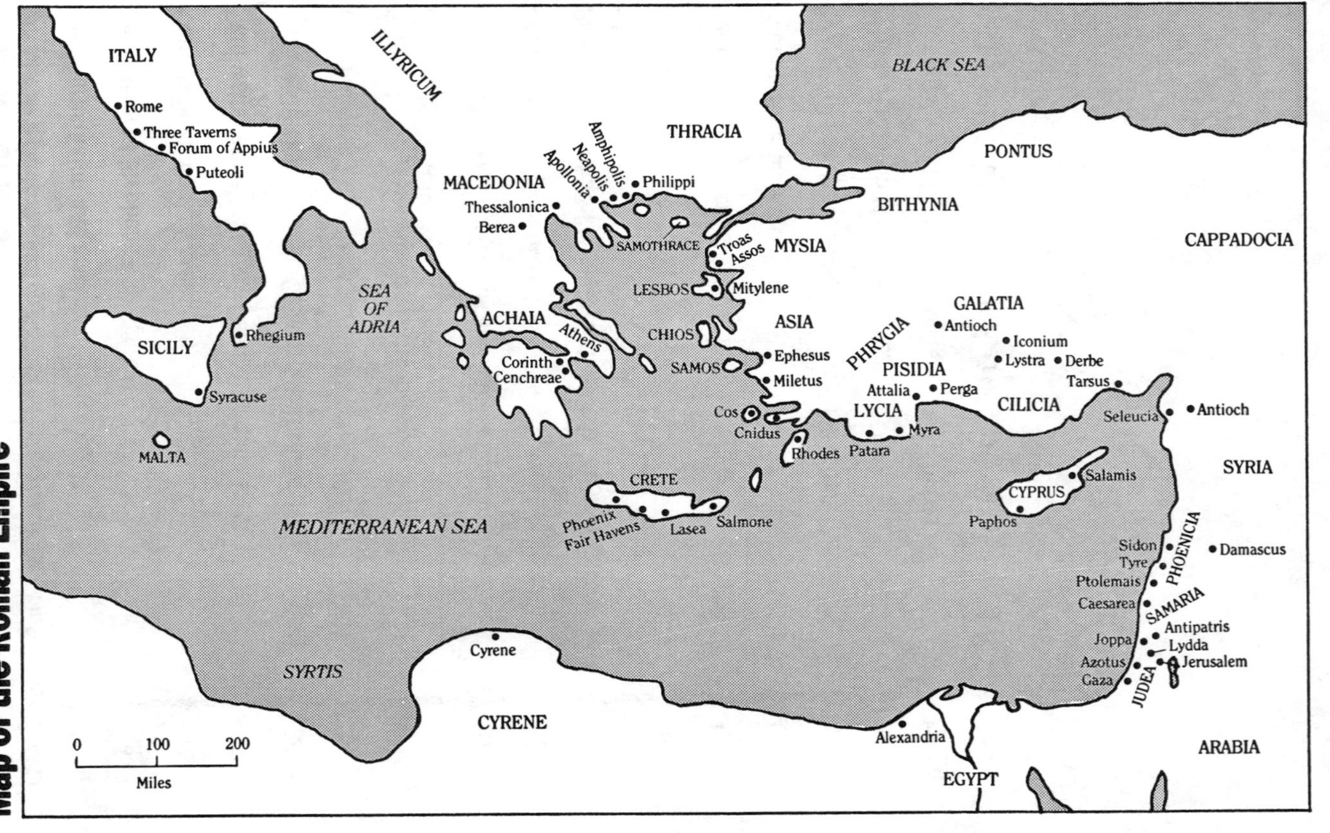

LESSON TWO

# ACTS 1:1-26

## Preparation

Luke was a master of many styles of writing. He wrote Luke 1:1-4 in formal, classical Greek, but in the rest of his Gospel and all of Acts, Luke used a style reminiscent of the Septuagint, the Greek version of the Old Testament.

Septuagint Greek was a unique style. It was almost as different from the Greek spoken in Luke's day as the English of the King James Bible is different from what is spoken today. Why did Luke use the style of the Jewish Bible? Perhaps he knew he was writing "sacred history,"[1] a continuation of God's dealings with man that began in Genesis and reached its culmination in the ministry of Jesus. By using the Septuagint's style and quoting it often, Luke stressed that Acts recounted the continuation and fulfillment of the Scripture's story.

Before you begin the questions in this lesson, read 1:1-26 all the way through. You might find it helpful to compare two versions of the Bible. Ask God to show you the important truths of this opening chapter of Acts.

**Study Skill—Outlining**

Sketching a rough outline of a chapter is often good preparation for studying it closely. It is also often helpful to relate the chapter to the themes of the whole book. Then, after studying the chapter in detail, you can reconsider your outline and how the chapter relates to the whole.

1. For each of the following sections, write a title that expresses what the section is about.

   1:1-11 ______________________________

   ______________________________

   1:12-26 ______________________________

   ______________________________

2. If Acts tells how the Church began to fulfill its mission through the Holy Spirit, how does 1:1-26 relate to this theme?

   ______________________________

   ______________________________

   ______________________________

   ______________________________

## Commission (1:1-11)

***Apostles*** (1:2). An apostle is literally "one who is sent"—a messenger, proxy, ambassador. In Jewish law, an *apostolos* (Greek) or *shaliach* (Aramaic) was "a person acting with full authority for another" in a business or legal transaction.[2] John 13:16,20 and 20:21 reflect the Jewish idea of the *shaliach*.

During His earthly life, Jesus appointed twelve of His disciples to be His apostles (Luke 6:12-16). To these twelve He gave the most intensive training and intimate friendship.

The early Church eventually recognized other believers as apostles in some sense: Paul (Acts 14:14), Barnabas (Acts 14:14), James the brother of Jesus (Galatians 1:19), and perhaps Andronicus and Junias (Romans 16:7). However, it is not clear that all these people held the Church's highest authority regarding doctrine and policy, as the Twelve did.[3] Paul does seem to have eventually attained this status (Galatians 1:1-2:10). Nevertheless, in these early chapters of Acts, Luke uses the term "the Twelve" as equivalent to "the apostles."

***Kingdom of God*** (1:3). Jesus called His message "the good news of the kingdom of God" (Luke 4:43), and He spoke about the Kingdom constantly. The Old Testament had promised that God would restore His own kingship over the earth, and Jesus proclaimed that the Kingdom was present in the person of the King, Jesus Himself. The early Church spoke of the Kingdom to refer to "the saving, sovereign action of God through" Jesus (Acts 8:12; 19:8; 20:25; 28:23,31).[4]

The Jews believed that when the *Messiah* (God's "Anointed One") came, He would inaugurate God's Kingdom on earth by delivering Israel from its oppressors. One of the prophesied signs of the Kingdom was that God would pour out His Spirit (Isaiah 44:3, Joel 2:28-32). Jesus' disciples knew He was the Messiah (Greek: *Christ*), so they supposed that by promising the Spirit, Jesus was saying He would soon ***restore the kingdom to Israel*** (Acts 1:6). Despite Jesus' teaching, they still thought He was going to establish a political kingdom at once.

**For Further Study:** Using a concordance (see page 214), trace what Jesus says about the Kingdom of God in one of the Gospels.

**For Thought and Discussion:** What do we need to know about the time of Jesus' return (Luke 21:5-36, especially verses 8-9,34-36; and Acts 1:11)? What don't we need to know (Acts 1:7)? Why is this distinction important for us to remember?

3. From Acts 1:2-5, what was apparently the purpose of the forty days Jesus spent with His disciples after the Resurrection?

______________________________

______________________________

______________________________

______________________________

***Baptized*** (1:5). Literally, "to immerse a person in water or to deluge him with it, usually as a means of cleansing."[5] The Old Testament often describes the Holy Spirit figuratively as a liquid that can be "poured out" (Isaiah 44:3, Joel 2:28). However, Scripture also speaks of the Spirit filling and coming upon people. We should remember that these terms are figurative; the Spirit is a Person, not a fluid or a force like electricity.

**Optional Application:** Does 1:8 apply to you? If not, why not? If so, what are some attitudes, priorities, or specific actions that this verse suggests for your life.

**For Thought and Discussion:** How was it going to be possible for the apostles to fulfill their mission (1:8)? Why is this important for us to remember?

**Optional Application:** Does 1:11 encourage you? If so, what does it encourage you to think and do?

4. Consider what Jesus said to the apostles when they asked whether His reign in power was about to begin (1:6-8). Why wasn't it important for the apostles to know precisely when Jesus would finish bringing God's reign to earth?

5. Why was it necessary for Jesus to stop giving direct instructions to His disciples and ascend to be with His Father (Acts 1:9)? See John 16:5-15.

6. a. What conviction was going to sustain the apostles as they fulfilled their mission while Jesus was physically absent (1:11)?

   b. Why would this have been encouraging?

## A twelfth witness chosen (1:12-26)

***A Sabbath day's walk*** (1:12). Jewish tradition said that traveling more than 3000 feet was work, so that distance came to be called a Sabbath day's journey.[6]

***Women*** (1:14). Among these were probably the wives of the apostles, as well as Jesus' mother. But unlike most Jewish teachers, Jesus had permitted women to travel with Him as disciples and even support Him financially; those women were among the witnesses to His crucifixion and resurrection (Mark 15:40-41; Luke 8:1-3; 23:49,55-56; 24:1-11).

***Brothers*** (1:14). When the Church came to believe that Mary remained a virgin throughout her life, it was assumed that Jesus' "brothers" were either His cousins or Joseph's sons by a previous marriage. However, some people think they were the sons of Joseph and Mary, Jesus' half brothers. They did not believe He was the Son of God during His life, so they continually tried to dissuade Him from the path that appeared insane (Mark 3:21, John 7:5). But Jesus appeared to them after His resurrection, and they believed. The eldest brother, James, became a leader in the Jerusalem church (Acts 12:17, 15:13; Galatians 2:9).

At His death, Jesus committed His mother into the care of the Apostle John, since His brothers did not yet believe (John 19:26-27). From this fact, and because Joseph is not mentioned in Acts 1:14, we conclude that he had died.

***In their language*** (1:19). Verses 18-19 are a parenthesis that Luke has inserted into Peter's speech to explain to the reader how Judas died. Peter's words actually flow from 1:17 to 1:20.[7]

***It is necessary*** (1:21). According to Jewish law, a hundred and twenty or more adult men could establish a community with its own ruling council. The ***hundred and twenty*** (1:15) believers were going to set up their own community with the twelve apostles as its council.[8]

Twelve men were necessary because they symbolized the twelve patriarchs who headed the twelve tribes (the whole nation) of Israel. (See Matthew 19:28, where "judging" is the Hebrew term for ruling or governing.[9]) Just as the patriarchs were the heads (under God) of Israel, so the apostles are the heads (under Jesus) of the Church.

7. How did Peter describe the chief function of an apostle (1:22)? What were the qualifications of such a person (1:21-22)?

_______________________________________________

_______________________________________________

_______________________________________________

_______________________________________________

_______________________________________________

_______________________________________________

_______________________________________________

***Justus*** (1:23). Many Jews had both a Hebrew and a Greek or Latin name. "Joseph" is Hebrew; "Justus" is Latin. "Barsabbas" means "son of the Sabbath"; many Jews had nicknames that began "son of . . ." (4:36, 13:6).

***Ministry*** (1:25). "The Greek word *diakonia* means 'service' (originally service at a meal table), and it is used of Christian work of all kinds, which takes its pattern from the One who came not to be served but to serve (Mark 10:45)."[10] "To serve tables" in 6:2 (NASB) is *diakonoi*; this is the root of the English word *deacon*.

***Lots*** (1:26). This method of discerning God's will for a decision was common in Old Testament times and among the Jews. Proverbs 16:33 states the belief that God, not chance, determined the outcome when lots were cast. Acts 1:26 is the only biblical instance of Christians casting lots.

8. a. What role did prayer have among the believers between the Ascension and Pentecost (1:14,24-25)?

______________________________

______________________________

______________________________

b. How is this a model for us?

______________________________

______________________________

______________________________

______________________________

**For Further Study:** Trace references to prayer in Acts. Who prays? Why? What happens when people pray? What do your observations imply for your life?

## Your response

9. Acts covers many topics that are relevant to our lives. On pages 32-34, some of the book's themes are given with space for you to write what you learn about each theme as you go through the book. For now, look back over this lesson and 1:1-26, and write what you can about each theme on pages 32-34. Give verse references for your observations.

**Study Skill—Application**

Because Acts is a narrative (a true story), it teaches us mainly by example, not directly as the Gospels and Epistles do. However, the first thirty years of Church history were a unique period in the history of God's dealings with man. Therefore, not everything in Acts sets an example that we should imitate. Acts records what *did* happen, not necessarily what should have happened or what always should happen. (For instance, the apostles cast lots and prayed to select the twelfth apostle, 1:23-26. Is this meant to be a model for choosing an apostle, or leaders in general? How do we know?)

*(continued on page 28)*

*(continued from page 27)*

To apply Acts to our lives sensibly, we need to distinguish when Luke is describing an example we *should* follow; when he is describing one we *may* follow; and when he is giving details to portray the *overall message,* not to be exact models for us.

One clue to this distinction is that *primary patterns recur* whereas *specific details vary.* For instance, people repeatedly pray for God's guidance to make decisions in Acts, but casting lots occurs only once, before the Spirit is poured out at Pentecost. Likewise, when people become believers in Acts, water baptism and the gift of the Holy Spirit normally occur, but "these can be in reverse order, with or without the laying on of hands, with or without the mention of tongues, and scarcely ever with a specific mention of repentance, even after what Peter says in 2:38-39."[11]

You'll find more guidelines for application later in this study guide. For now, keep this question in mind: When is a practice in Acts a norm we should follow, when is it an option we should consider, and when is it unique to the time? Also, watch for recurring patterns and varying details.

10. Review your answers to questions 4, 5, 8, and 9. Ask God to guide you, and write down a) the one specific truth from 1:1-26 you want to take to heart; and b) any commitment to some action or prayer you would like to make during the coming week.

    a. ______________________________

    ______________________________

    ______________________________

    b. ______________________________

    ______________________________

    ______________________________

**Study Skill—Outlining**

Some people remember a book better if they outline it as they go through it. Questions 1 and 2 of this lesson have given you a head start on outlining chapter 1 of Acts. If you like, start with a broad framework, such as one of those on page 12. Then add specifics:

1:1-26 ______________________

______________________

1:1-5 ______________________

______________________

1:6-11 ______________________

______________________

1:12-26 ______________________

______________________

Give each section a title that tells what it is about. Try to show how the sections contribute to the themes of Acts.

11. If you have any questions about 1:1-26, write them here.

______________________

______________________

______________________

______________________

## For the group

**Worship.**

**Warm-up.** Instead of launching right into the study, it is often helpful to begin with a simple question related to the theme of the lesson. This helps people unwind from the day's business and focus on the Scripture. A warm-up question for Acts 1:1-26 might be, "What is a witness?"

**Read aloud.** It is usually a good idea to read aloud the passage you are going to study. This refreshes everyone's memory and, like the warm-up, helps everyone to focus.

**Summarize.** Ask someone to summarize what 1:1-26 is about. A quick summary at the beginning can keep you from losing sight of the forest when you examine the trees. Questions 1 and 2 may help.

**Discussion.** Sometimes, in order to make a question clearer or just to make the discussion more interesting, you may want to rephrase a question in the study guide. If you want to do this, keep in mind that most questions ask you either to *observe* what a passage says, *interpret* what it means, or *apply* it to yourselves.

Also, you may sometimes need to ask a few questions about the word definitions and background in the lesson, such as "what does 'so-and-so' mean?" Make sure that everyone understands important words, but don't worry if many people aren't interested in all the details. The background is there to help the book come alive for you, but you don't have to memorize all of it.

Talk about the Study Skill on pages 27-28. Does everyone understand the differences between a norm we must follow, an option we may follow, and a unique event that is not an example for us? How does this distinction apply to Acts 1:1-26?

Many groups feel that half their discussion time should be devoted to exploring how the passage applies to their lives. If you've prepared the interpretation questions ahead of time, you should not need long to cover them. But even if you decide to spend less than half of your time on application, do allow at least fifteen minutes for it. Don't *insist* that members do something about the passage, but do *encourage* them to do so; ask what difference it should make to their lives. You could suggest that each member tell one person outside the group one significant insight he or she had from your discussion. Or, suggest that a member choose an insight or several verses to meditate on for the next week. Not everyone may feel comfortable telling what he or she plans to do for application. You may need to make an effort to develop trust and openness over several weeks.

Make sure that everyone understands the point of pages 32-34. Discuss what you learned about the Church's mission, the Holy Spirit, etc. from 1:1-26. Encourage the group to keep up with these lists, since when finished they will give you illuminating topical studies of Acts.

Give everyone a chance to raise questions about the passage.

**Summarize.** Ask one person or several people to summarize the main points of your discussion. What do you want to remember from 1:1-26? Summarizing a discussion helps to clarify it in people's minds so they can remember it. Pull together what 1:1-26 is about and also how it applies to you.

**Worship.** Thank Jesus for giving His Church its mission and promising power to accomplish that mission. Thank Him for preparing the apostles to be His witnesses. Give thanks for the return He promised.

1. Marshall, page 18.
2. Erich von Eicken and Helgo Lindner, "Apostle," *The New International Dictionary of New Testament Theology,* volume 1, edited by Colin Brown (Grand Rapids, Michigan: Zondervan Corporation, 1975), page 128.
3. *The NIV Study Bible,* page 1505.
4. Marshall, page 57.
5. Marshall, page 58.
6. H. Porter, "Sabbath Day's Journey," *The International Standard Bible Encyclopaedia,* volume 4, edited by James Orr (Grand Rapids, Michigan: William B. Eerdmans Publishing Company, 1956), page 2634.
7. *The NIV Study Bible,* page 1645 and Marshall, pages 64-65, explain ways of harmonizing Acts 1:18-19 with Matthew 27:3-8.
8. Marshall, page 64.
9. *The NIV Study Bible,* page 1470; "Krino" in Geoffrey W. Bromiley, *Theological Dictionary of the New Testament* abridged in one volume, edited by Gerhard Kittel and Gerhard Friedrich (Grand Rapids, Michigan: William B. Eerdmans Publishing Company, 1985), pages 469-473.
10. Marshall, page 66.
11. Fee and Stuart, page 92.

What is the Church's mission?

What is the Church's message?

What is the the Holy Spirit's role in the Church and the world?

How do believers respond to opposition and persecution in Acts?

What is the relationship between Christianity and Judaism in Acts?

---

What does Acts show about fellowship
(partnership, participation, sharing, communion)?

---

LESSON THREE

# ACTS 2:1-41

## Pentecost

Forty days after the Resurrection, Jesus left His disciples with a mission and a promise. For ten more days the believers prayed together and prepared. Then came the Jewish feast of Pentecost.

Read 2:1-41 before you begin the questions. Imagine yourself as one of the believers gathered to celebrate the feast with no idea of what was coming. Or, put yourself in the crowd of Jews witnessing the bizarre events and Peter's speech. Ask God to bring this scene alive for you.

**For Thought and Discussion:** Briefly, what is 2:1-41 about?

### The Spirit descends (2:1-13)

***Pentecost*** (2:1). The fiftieth day after the Sabbath of Passover week (*pente koste* is Greek for "fiftieth day"). *Pentecost* is the name Greek-speaking Jews used for the Feast of Weeks (Leviticus 23:15-21, Deuteronomy 16:9-12), the Feast of Harvest (Exodus 23:16), or the Day of Firstfruits (Numbers 28:26-31). On Pentecost, the Jews brought offerings of the firstfruits of the wheat harvest to the Temple to thank the Lord for it. In Jesus' time, Pentecost "was associated with the renewal of the covenant made with Noah and then with Moses . . . ; in second-century Judaism Pentecost was regarded as the day when the law was given at Sinai."[1]

**For Thought and Discussion:** Pentecost was the only time in Acts when the Spirit came with windlike sound and firelike appearance. What might have been the point of these outward signs?

1. Why was it appropriate that the events of Acts 2 occurred on Pentecost, the day when Jews celebrated the giving of the covenant under the Law of Moses? (*Optional:* See Jeremiah 31:31-34, Romans 7:6, 2 Corinthians 3:6.)

______________________________________

______________________________________

______________________________________

______________________________________

______________________________________

**Study Skill—Metaphors and Similes**

*Metaphors* and *similes* are figures of speech. They shed light on something by referring to it as something else in order to imply a comparison between the two. A metaphor compares by saying something *is* another ("You are the salt of the earth"). A simile uses the words *like* or *as* to show the comparison.

In Acts 2:2-3, Luke describes the sound of the Spirit as "*like* the blowing of a violent wind" and His visible effect as "what seemed to be tongues of fire" ("tongues *as* of fire" in RSV and NASB). Wind (2 Samuel 22:16; Job 37:10; Ezekiel 37:9,14; John 3:8) and fire (Exodus 3:2, 19:18; Luke 3:16) are common biblical symbols for the presence of God's Spirit.[2] The Greek word *pneuma* and the Hebrew *ruach* mean both "wind" and "spirit."

---

***Filled with the Holy Spirit*** (2:4). Luke uses the word *filled* "when people are given an initial endowment of the Spirit to fit them for God's service" (Luke 1:15, Acts 9:17) "and also when they are inspired to make important utterances" (Acts 4:8,31; 13:9). "Related words are used to describe the continuous process of being filled with the Spirit" (Acts 13:52, Ephesians 5:18) "or the corresponding state of being full" (Luke 4:1; Acts 6:3,5; 7:55; 11:24). "These references indicate that a person already filled with the

Spirit can receive a fresh filling for a specific task, or a continuous filling."[3]

To be "baptized" (Acts 1:5, 11:16) with the Spirit is the same as the initial filling the disciples received at Pentecost. However, the recurring experience is always called filling, never baptism.[4]

***God-fearing Jews from every nation*** (2:5). Devout Jews tried to get to Jerusalem for the three main feasts of the year: Passover, Pentecost, and Tabernacles (Deuteronomy 16:16). Also, Jews who came from other parts of the world often moved to Judea in their old age in order to die in the promised land. Therefore, at Pentecost Jerusalem was full of Jews and *proselytes* (converts to Judaism) from all over the Mediterranean world and the Middle East.

Most of them would have understood the Aramaic language (similar to Hebrew) spoken in Palestine and the Greek spoken all over the known world. However, each Jew also had a native language which almost no one from elsewhere was likely to know.

---

**For Thought and Discussion:** a. How do you know if you are filled with the Spirit (Romans 8:9-10, Ephesians 1:13-14)?

b. How should being Spirit-filled affect what you do? (See, for example, Acts 1:8, Romans 8:5-8, 1 Corinthians 12:12-26, 2 Corinthians 3:17-4:12, Galatians 5:16-26.) Should you do everything the apostles did? Why or why not?

2. What were the "other tongues" (2:4) that the Holy Spirit enabled the disciples to speak (2:6,11)?

________________________________________

________________________________________

________________________________________

________________________________________

---

***Too much wine*** (2:13). A Jew from Phrygia, for instance, may have heard one or two of the disciples speaking Phrygian. However, the disciples speaking Mede or Cyrenian would have been unintelligible and may have seemed to be babbling drunkenly.

Four interpretations of the languages have been offered: 1) in Acts 2 they are the human languages of the various nations, but in 1 Cor-

**For Thought and Discussion:** Is Peter's speech in 2:14-40 a model for our evangelism in any ways? If so, which elements should we remember to teach others? Why is each element important?

**For Further Study:** Outline Peter's speech by giving titles to 2:14-21, 2:22-24, 2:25-32, 2:33-35, 2:36, and 2:37-40. What key points does Peter make in each section?

inthians 12-14 they are non-human, heavenly languages; 2) both Acts and 1 Corinthians refer to human languages not known to the speaker; 3) both Acts and 1 Corinthians refer to non-human languages; 4) 1 Corinthians alludes to languages both of "men" and of "angels" (13:1), while Acts portrays only the languages of "men" not known to the speaker.

## Peter speaks (2:14-41)

Peter realizes that the promise of Acts 1:8 is being fulfilled, so he seizes the chance to begin fulfilling his mission. Notice the points he makes in his speech.

**Study Skill—Old Testament Quotations**

If you compare the Old Testament quotations in Acts with the same passages in your Bible's Old Testament, you will notice differences for several reasons:

1. New Testament writers and speakers often give "the general sense" of a passage rather than quoting it word for word.
2. They often quote from the *Septuagint*, the Greek translation of the Old Testament which was used by many Jews.
3. A New Testament writer or speaker sometimes enlarges, abbreviates, or adapts an Old Testament passage, or combines two or more passages to make his point. The Holy Spirit has inspired these adaptations just as He has inspired the rest of the New Testament.[5]

***In the last days*** (2:17). The Hebrew of Joel 2:28 says "afterward," but Peter interprets the time "afterward" refers to. Jews divide history into two periods: this world or age, and the world or age to come. The end of this age and the beginning of the age to come is marked by the ***day of the Lord*** (Acts 2:20) when God will send His Messiah, vanquish His enemies, and inaugurate the new covenant (Isaiah 2:1-5; Jeremiah 31:31-34; Ezekiel 36:26-27, 39:29; Joel 1:15).[6] Peter says the last days have begun and the day of the Lord is imminent.

---

3. Peter says that the babble of languages is a sign of something greater than drunkenness. What does the sign demonstrate (2:15-21)?

_______________

_______________

_______________

_______________

_______________

4. Next Peter recounts the key facts of Jesus' life (2:22-24).

   a. How could the Jews have known that Jesus was a special person sent by God (2:22)?

   _______________

   _______________

   _______________

   b. How did Israel respond to Jesus (2:23)?

   _______________

   _______________

   _______________

   c. What was the crucial event of Jesus' career, and what did it prove (2:24,36)? (Notice that the word *therefore* in 2:36 points to the conclusion of Peter's reasoning in 2:22-36.)

   _______________

   _______________

   _______________

   _______________

**For Thought and Discussion:** Peter addresses his first sermon to Jews (Acts 2:5,14,22). Why is this important for us to remember? (Recall 1:8.)

**For Thought and Discussion:** The Holy Spirit empowered the apostles to proclaim the gospel. Are you empowered and equipped for evangelism? If so, how can you use that power? If not, should you be equipped, and how can you be equipped?

**Optional Application:** Is 2:22-24 a helpful framework for your evangelism? Could you explain these facts to someone who didn't know the gospel? If not, how can you become able to do so?

***Christ*** (2:31). This key word appears here for the first time in Acts. To Jews, it was a title: the Anointed One, the Messiah, the king and descendant of David promised in the Scriptures. Psalm 16, which Peter quoted in Acts 2:25-28, was already considered a prophecy of the Christ.

***Lord . . . Lord*** (2:34). The original Hebrew has different words. The first "Lord" is *YHWH,* the name of God, rendered "LORD" in the NIV of Psalm 110:1. The Jews felt that *YHWH* was too holy to be pronounced, so they said *Adon* ("Lord") instead. The second "Lord" is *Adon,* which means "lord" or "master."

The Hebrew of Psalm 110:1 makes it clear that the LORD (God) is speaking to David's Lord (the Messiah), but the Greek of Acts 2:34 uses the same word for both. Therefore, when Peter calls Jesus "Lord" in 2:36, it's not obvious whether he means that Jesus is just the Messiah or also God.

5. How did the Resurrection prove that Jesus is . . .

   Christ (2:25-33)? ______________________

   Lord (2:34-35)? ______________________

6. According to Peter, what does Jesus have to do with the miraculous speaking the Jews have heard (2:16,33)?

______________________________________________

______________________________________________

______________________________________________

______________________________________________

______________________________________________

______________________________________________

7. Hearing all this, the Jews are "cut to the heart" (2:37). Why would Peter's message (2:22-24,36) affect a Jewish audience like this?

______________________________________________

______________________________________________

______________________________________________

______________________________________________

______________________________________________

______________________________________________

**For Thought and Discussion:** Why didn't Peter have to prove that Jesus had done miracles (2:22)? How can this fact help us to convince modern people that Jesus did miracles?

**For Thought and Discussion:** Why does Peter mention God's plan and foreknowledge in 2:23? Why is it important for us to remember?

---

***Repent*** (2:38). "The word indicates a change of direction in a person's life rather than simply a mental change of attitude or a feeling of remorse; it signifies a turning away from a sinful and godless way of life. In one sense this is something of which man is incapable by himself, and therefore, although men can be commanded to repent, it can also be said that repentance is a gift of God (Acts 5:31, 11:18; 2 Timothy 2:25)." Repentance "is an essential part of conversion."[7]

***Baptized . . . in the name of Jesus Christ*** (2:38). A public declaration of allegiance to Jesus as the Christ and commitment to Him as one's own Lord. In commerce and popular speech, "in the name of" meant "to the account of" or "with

**For Thought and Discussion:** Peter tried to convince Jews about Jesus by showing how scriptures they *already accepted* supported his claims. Would this approach work with your friends? Why or why not? If not, what beliefs that you *already hold in common* could you use to draw them toward examining the Scriptures?

**For Thought and Discussion:** To what extent were the events of Pentecost a precedent that describes what we should do, believe, and experience when we become Christians? How can we decide this? How typical is Pentecost of other conversions in Acts?

reference to."[8] Paul used the phrase to mean "into union with" and "into commitment to" (Romans 6:2-5).

This baptismal formula does not contradict the fuller one in Matthew 28:19. For Jews, who already believed in the Father and the Holy Spirit, the new commitment was to Jesus as Lord and Christ.

8. What will God do for the person who makes the inner commitment of repentance and the outer declaration of baptism (Acts 2:38)?

______________________________

______________________________

______________________________

______________________________

***With many other words*** (2:40). Luke explains that 2:14-39 is only a summary of Peter's speech. He probably spoke much longer than the few minutes it would have taken to say these verses. Many of the speeches in Acts are probably summaries like this one.[9]

***Three thousand*** (2:41). Many of those new believers may have returned the next day to other parts of the Roman world, taking the gospel with them.

## Your response

9. The sermons in Acts suggest outlines we can follow in explaining the good news to others. Summarize what Peter asks the Jews to *believe* and *do*, and *why* they should do these things.

truths to believe (2:21-24,31-33,36,39)

______________________________

______________________________

______________________________

actions to do (2:21,38)

reasons why (2:20-21,38,40)

10. What one insight from 2:1-41 would you most like to take to heart?

11. How does this insight apply to you? (For instance, is there some promise or command addressed to all believers that you can act on more fully than you are? Does some truth about Jesus have implications for your attitudes and actions? How do you fall short with regard to your insight?)

**Optional Application:** What difference should what Peter told the Jews make to your attitudes and actions?

**Optional Application:** To whom can you tell Peter's message? Ask God to show you.

**Optional Application:** Thank God for what He did at Pentecost. Ask Him to give you as vivid a conviction of the Spirit's presence in your life as He gave the early believers. Ask Him to show you how to act on the power the Spirit gives you.

**Optional Application:** Ask God how you can treat Jesus as Lord and Christ more fully. Ask Him if there is any area of your life in which you need to repent.

**For Further Study:** Using questions 1 and 13 and the subtitles in this lesson, add 2:1-41 to your outline of Acts.

12. What action can you take (including prayer) to begin putting this insight into practice this week?

13. What does 2:1-41 contribute to the overall message of Acts? (See 1:8 and your answer to question 7 on page 14.)

14. On pages 32-34, jot down what 2:1-41 reveals about the Church's mission and message, the role of the Holy Spirit, etc.

15. List any questions you have about 2:1-41.

## For the group

**Warm-up.** Ask the group, "Have you ever tried to explain the gospel to someone? What happened? How did you feel?"

**Read aloud and summarize.**

**The Spirit descends.** Christians disagree as to how normative the events of Pentecost are for what modern believers should experience. We can get some clues if we compare the experiences Cornelius' household had at conversion (10:24-48). However, some people maintain that what those early converts experienced is always different from what believers experience today, while other people say that the experiences should always be the same. Still others say we should expect some but not all converts to have Acts-like experiences. To avoid a debate on this, state these various opinions and concentrate on issues you can agree on and apply practically.

One practical issue is whether you are filled with the Spirit as the disciples were. How do you know whether you are or aren't? If you aren't, should you be, and why? If you are, how should that affect what you do? Do you have the power to spread the gospel as they did? Why or why not? This is a knotty problem for many people, for we may believe intellectually that we are filled with the Spirit, yet we may not be doing what we think a Spirit-filled person ought to be doing. The matter is more complicated because "Spirit-filled" means different things to different people.

**Peter speaks.** Use question 9 to organize your discussion of Peter's speech. Instead of discussing questions 3-8 one by one, you can simply lead the group into a thorough answer to question 9. Outlining the speech (see the "For Further Study" on page 38) may also help the group follow Peter's train of thought.

Applications of 2:14-41 should be easier than ones of 2:1-13, since 2:1-13 is arguably a unique event in the history of the Church. Encourage each group member to come up with one insight to apply in prayer and action.

You might try applying the passage together. For example, the Spirit equipped the disciples to preach the gospel. Are you equipped? What can you do together to become equipped and then actually share the gospel with others? You may not be called to Peter's brand of public evangelism, but you may learn to explain the good news to individuals and small groups of friends. You can even commit yourselves to pray for each other to find opportunities to display the gospel.

If you don't feel ready to tell the gospel, how can you live as though you really believe what Peter says? What difference do his teachings make to your thoughts and actions?

**Summarize.** What are the main things you learned from your discussion of 2:1-41?

**Wrap-up.** Lesson six deals with the inner workings of the Jerusalem church as described in 2:42-47, 4:32-5:11, and 6:1-7. Explain this to anyone who wonders why lesson three skips 2:42-47.

**Worship.** Praise God for sending Jesus, allowing Him to be crucified, raising Him from death, and exalting Him to honor. Thank Him for foretelling Jesus' coming and the last days through the prophets. Thank Him for sending the Spirit. Praise Jesus as Lord and Christ, and thank Him for offering you forgiveness. Pray for those you know who have never called on the Lord to be saved from destruction, and ask God to empower you with His Spirit to spread the gospel.

1. Marshall, page 68.
2. Marshall, page 68.
3. Marshall, page 69.
4. Marshall, page 69; Homer A. Kent, Jr., *Jerusalem to Rome: Studies in the Book of Acts* (Grand Rapids, Michigan: Baker Book House, 1972), page 30.
5. *The NIV Study Bible,* page 1709.
6. William Barclay, *The Acts of the Apostles,* revised edition (Philadelphia: Westminster Press, 1976), page 25.
7. Marshall, pages 80-81.
8. Marshall, page 81.
9. Marshall, page 82.

LESSON FOUR

# ACTS 3:1-26

## Miracle

As Jesus promised (John 14:26, Acts 1:8), the Father sent the Holy Spirit to empower the apostles to witness. As you read 3:1-26, consider what aspects of the story are unique to that time, and what aspects are relevant to our lives today.

**For Further Study:** **Briefly summarize what happens in 3:1-10 and 3:11-26.**

### Healing (3:1-10)

***At the time of prayer*** (3:1). Nine a.m. (the third hour), three p.m. (the ninth hour), and sunset were the standard times of prayer.[1]

***Beautiful*** (3:2). Probably the Nicanor Gate, the bronze-covered one from the Court of the Gentiles to the Court of the Women.[2]

***Beg*** (3:2). Giving alms was considered a good deed that merited God's blessing. However, people normally just dropped coins into a beggar's hand without any personal contact.

***In the name of Jesus Christ*** (3:6). A different Greek phrase from that in 2:38. This one means "by the authority of Jesus."[3] See 3:16, 4:10.

1. How does Acts 3:1-10 reflect Jesus' words in John 14:12-14?

**For Thought and Discussion:** How does the former cripple respond to his healing (3:8)? Is there an example here for us? Compare Luke 17:11-19.

**Optional Application:** Have you experienced any kind of healing by Jesus' power? If so, how should that affect what you do?

______________________________

______________________________

______________________________

2. The beggar asked for money (3:3), but Peter and John met quite a different need.

   a. What was the relationship between physical healing and spiritual salvation in Jesus' work and teaching? (*Optional:* See Luke 4:18-19, 5:17-26, 7:20-23, 9:1-2.)

   ______________________________

   ______________________________

   ______________________________

   ______________________________

   b. What purposes did the physical healing serve in Acts 3? (See Acts 3:8-13,16; 4:4-14.)

   ______________________________

   ______________________________

   ______________________________

   ______________________________

   ______________________________

   ______________________________

   c. Why do you think Peter and John healed the beggar physically instead of just either giving him money or offering him spiritual salvation?

   ______________________________

   ______________________________

   ______________________________

   ______________________________

   ______________________________

   ______________________________

3. Does 3:1-10 set any example for our priorities or mission today? If so, how? If not, why not?

**For Thought and Discussion:** What would be the advantages and disadvantages of attracting people to Jesus by means of miracles?

**For Thought and Discussion:** Even if we don't perform miraculous healings, how is 3:1-10 relevant to us?

## Peter speaks (3:11-26)

***Solomon's Colonnade*** (3:11). The porch that ran along the east side of the Court of the Gentiles. It had "rows of 27-foot-high stone columns and a roof of cedar."[4] It was a good thirty yards wide and over five hundred yards long, so there was plenty of room for large gatherings (5:12).

***Our own power or godliness*** (3:12). The Jews apparently assumed that Peter and John must either have superhuman power or be "so devout that God would respond to their prayers with miraculous signs."[5]

4. According to Peter, how was this healing possible (3:16)?

5. Why is it important for us that the apostles did not need their own power or exceptional godliness to heal the beggar (3:12)?

**Optional Application:** Explain to someone what it means that Jesus is God's Servant. Use Isaiah 52:13-53:12 and Acts 3:13-18. Also, explain to that person what difference it means to you personally that Jesus is the Servant whom Isaiah foretold.

**For Thought and Discussion:** Summarize the main points Peter makes in this speech to the Jews (3:11-26).

**For Thought and Discussion:** The Crucifixion signified God's curse (Galatians 3:13). Still, what event proved that God regarded Jesus as holy and righteous, not accursed (Acts 3:15)?

6. How did Peter describe Jesus in this speech (3:13-15,22)?

______________________________________

______________________________________

______________________________________

______________________________________

______________________________________

***Servant*** (3:13). A king's special minister or ambassador was often called his "servant" in ancient times. In the Old Testament, only God's special envoys are called His servants, such as Moses (Exodus 14:31), David (2 Samuel 3:18), and the prophets (2 Kings 17:13). Isaiah prophesied that a Servant of the Lord would come (Isaiah 42:1-9, 49:1-7, 50:4-9, 52:13-53:12). By calling Jesus God's "servant" whom He "glorified" but people "disowned" (Acts 3:13), Peter was alluding to Isaiah 52:13-53:12.

***Holy and Righteous One*** (3:14). Jesus was dedicated to God (holy) and morally upright (righteous). Peter proved this by pointing out Pilate's desire to release Jesus as innocent (3:13). For the Jews, it would have seemed incredible to call someone holy and righteous who had been hanged or impaled on a pole because Deuteronomy 21:22-23 said that this death signified God's curse.

7. In what senses is Jesus "the author of life" (Acts 3:15) or "the Prince of life" (KJV, NASB)? (*Optional:* See John 1:3-4,12-13; Colossians 1:15-23; Hebrews 2:14-15; 1 John 5:11-12.)

______________________________________

______________________________________

______________________________________

______________________________________

8. What does it mean that Jesus is God's Servant (Isaiah 52:13-53:12)?

_______________________________________

_______________________________________

_______________________________________

_______________________________________

_______________________________________

_______________________________________

_______________________________________

9. Because the Jews "acted in ignorance" when they disowned and killed Jesus, God will give them a second chance to repent (3:17). What will happen if they repent (3:19-21)?

_______________________________________

_______________________________________

_______________________________________

_______________________________________

_______________________________________

_______________________________________

***Repent . . . turn*** (3:19). In Hebrew, these come from the same root word. Repentance is turning the mind, will, and emotions *away from* sin; the turning that follows is therefore *toward* obedience, knowledge, and love of God.

## Your response

10. Peter tailored his speech for his fellow Jews, who had personally supported Jesus' execution, knew the Old Testament prophecies about the servant and the prophet like Moses, and had inherited the covenant.

**For Thought and Discussion:** a. What happens to any Jew who refuses to repent, turn, and listen to God's Prophet (Acts 3:22-23)? How is this relevant to us or to other people today?

b. How was the Jews' place in God's plan special (Acts 3:25-26)?

c. What do Peter's words tell you about the relationship between Christianity and Judaism? Write your answer on page 34.

**For Thought and Discussion:** How do we share the guilt for disowning and killing Jesus? What implications does this have for us?

**Optional Application:** Choose one of the things Peter says about Jesus in 3:11-26. How does this truth affect your life? Plan to think about this truth every day this week.

However, what parts of Peter's sermon could you include in explaining the gospel to unbelievers you know?

11. What truth in 3:1-26 seems most significant to you?

12. What implications does it have for your life? How does it make you want to change or respond?

13. What prayer and/or action can you take this week in light of this truth?

______________________________________________

______________________________________________

______________________________________________

______________________________________________

______________________________________________

______________________________________________

14. On pages 32-34, note what you've learned from 3:1-26 about the Church's mission and message and about the relationship between Christianity and Judaism.

15. List any questions you have about 3:1-26.

______________________________________________

______________________________________________

______________________________________________

______________________________________________

**For Further Study:** Add 3:1-26 to your outline, using question 1 to help you.

## For the group

If you prefer to move more slowly in order to allow more time for prayer and personal sharing, you can cover 3:1-10 and 3:11-26 in two meetings.

**Warm-up.** Ask everyone to think of how the Holy Spirit has been active in his or her life during the past week. (What has He been doing, and how can you tell?) Give everyone a chance to answer aloud if he or she wants to do so.

Or, discuss how your applications have been going. What have you been learning? Share your successes, insights, lessons, frustrations, and questions. Look for ways to encourage and help each other to apply Acts to your current decisions and circumstances.

**Healing.** Once again, the obvious issue 3:1-10 raises is whether the passage describes a unique event or a norm for today. Specifically, did the Holy Spirit empower miraculous healings only in the first century to get the Church started, or does He still do so today? Christians disagree strongly on this issue, so you may want to let everyone voice his opinion and move on. If you decide to discuss it at length, make sure that people give reasons for their views and don't hurt each other. Examine the merits of each point of view, and urge everyone to come to his or her own conclusions prayerfully.

Questions 1 and 2 are meant to lay a foundation for understanding what healing meant in Jesus' ministry. Even if you decide that miraculous healing itself is not part of your equipment for ministry, you can still find ways in which the healings are relevant to your lives.

**Peter speaks.** Some of what Peter says to the Jews doesn't apply to us, but it does tell us about the place of the Jews in God's plan. Also, what he says about Jesus is relevant to us—what difference does it make to you that Jesus is the Servant, the Holy and Righteous One, the Prophet, the Author (or Prince) of Life? This may be a more fruitful discussion than a debate about healing.

**Summarize.**

**Wrap-up.** Because lesson five is long, you may decide to omit parts of it or cover it in two meetings. Tell the group your plans ahead of time.

**Worship.** Praise Jesus as the Servant of the Lord, the Author of Life, the Prophet like Moses, the Holy and Righteous One. Thank God for sending first Jesus and then the Spirit to empower you.

1. *The NIV Study Bible,* page 1648.
2. *The NIV Study Bible,* page 1648; Marshall, pages 87-88.
3. Marshall, page 88.
4. *The NIV Study Bible,* page 1649.
5. Marshall, page 90.

LESSON FIVE

# ACTS 4:1-31, 5:12-42

## Confrontation

The Holy Spirit empowered the apostles to preach the gospel, speak in unknown languages, and even heal a lame man. Was this new Spirit-filled life all carefree fun? Read 4:1-31 and 5:12-42 prayerfully.

1. What happens in 4:1-31, and how is the passage connected to 3:1-26?

2. Briefly summarize 5:12-42.

## The Sanhedrin's first warning (4:1-22)

***Captain of the temple guard*** (4:1). Most ***priests*** worked in the Temple only two weeks a year and lived in the countryside the rest of the time. However, a few powerful families whose men were eligible to become high priests resided in Jerusalem. The captain of the temple police was a member of one of those families and ranked second to the high priest.[1]

***Sadducees*** (4:1). Most of the priests and elders (4:1,5) belonged to this political party or sect, including the chief priestly families from which the captain of the guard and the high priest were chosen. The Sadducees were wealthy, aristocratic Jews who supported Roman rule in exchange for Rome's protection of their power.[2]

Luke probably means that some of the lay elders accompanied the priestly Sadducees in seizing Peter and John.

***Jail*** (4:3). The Antonia Fortress was attached to the Temple and contained a prison.

***Evening*** (4:3). "The evening sacrifices ended about 4:00 P.M., and the temple gates would be closed at that time. Any judgments involving life and death must be begun and concluded in daylight hours" according to Jewish law.[3]

***Rulers, elders and teachers of the law*** (4:5). The three groups who composed the *Sanhedrin*, the high council that governed Jewish affairs. The rulers were probably the chief priests who held "various official positions in the administration of the temple." The elders "were the lay leaders of the community, no doubt the heads of the principal aristocratic families, mostly of Sadducean outlook."[4] The teachers of the law ("scribes" in RSV, NASB, KJV) interpreted and taught the rules and beliefs of Judaism according to their view of the Scriptures and the oral law. The teachers were mostly Pharisees.

The Pharisees and Sadducees were at odds for many reasons. The Sadducees were aristocrats and priests who considered the temple worship most important; most Pharisees belonged to the craftsman class and regarded the written and oral law above the temple ritual. The Pharisees considered the oral tradition (including teaching about angels and demons, the immortality of the soul, reward and punishment after death, and laws for behavior) as equal to the Scripture; the Sadducees accepted only the five books of Moses (Genesis-Deuteronomy), which they interpreted literally. The Pharisees awaited a Messiah to liberate Israel, inaugurate an age of peace and prosperity, and raise the dead; the Sadducees disbelieved in a personal Messiah and the resurrection, and they said that the Messianic age already existed. The Sadducees actively served and were supported by Rome; the Pharisees tolerated Rome but hoped for the Messiah.

The Sanhedrin was the recognized voice of God for the Jews; it was both the pastoral and the civil leadership.[5]

***Healed . . . saved*** (4:9,12). The Greek verb *sozo* means both to heal and to save.

***The stone . . . rejected*** (4:11). Psalm 118:22 may originally have meant that Israel (or Israel's king), whom the nations rejected, would prove to be the key nation or king in the world. Peter applies this saying about Israel or the king to Jesus.[6]

***Name*** (4:12). The name Jesus means "the Lord saves." However, for the Jews, the only name by which a person could be saved was *YHWH*, the holy, unpronounceable name of God (the LORD, see the note on page 40). Recall Peter's quotation of Joel 2:32 in Acts 2:21.

---

3. The Sanhedrin did not doubt that a healing had occurred; they only demanded to know by what authority (power or name, 4:7) the apostles were preaching and healing. Peter responded that his authority came from Jesus. Specifically what did Peter claim about Jesus (4:8-12)?

---

**For Thought and Discussion:** a. Why were the priests and other Sadducees so upset that the apostles were proclaiming Jesus resurrected (4:2, 23:8)?

b. The Sadducees did not believe in Jesus even though the healing was indisputable. Think about the Sadducees' beliefs, priorities, and values as reflected in John 11:47-53 and the background on pages 56-57. Why did they find it impossible to believe that Jesus was the Messiah?

c. What assumptions and priorities make it difficult for various groups of people today to accept Jesus even when they can't refute the evidence? How is it possible for these barriers to be overcome?

**For Thought and Discussion:** a. Peter and John were committed to obeying God rather than the Jewish leaders when commands conflicted (4:19). What had God commanded them to do (1:8)?

b. According to 4:19, under what circumstances must Christians disobey human authorities, and when must we obey human authorities?

c. Think of a modern situation in which a Christian should disobey the authorities and one in which he should obey.

**For Further Study:** a. How does Acts 4:1-22 reflect Jesus' teaching in Luke 12:11-12 and 21:12-19?

b. What does Peter say in 1 Peter 2:13-17 about how to treat human authorities? Does he follow those instructions in Acts?

c. What does Paul say in Romans 13:1-7 about this subject? Does Peter do in Acts what Paul teaches?

4. So far, Peter and John had done nothing wrong, and the Sanhedrin couldn't deny the miracle, so at this point they could only issue a command and a warning (4:13-18). How did Peter respond (4:19-20)?

5. What principles for Christian behavior before authorities do Peter and John exemplify (4:5-13,18-20)? (See also 5:29-32.)

## The believers' prayer (4:23-31)

6. How do the believers respond to the Sanhedrin's threats (4:23-31)?

7. What do they confess about God? Write down as many observations as you can (4:24-30).

8. What do they ask God to do (4:29-30)?

**For Thought and Discussion:** How can we be sure we are correct when we believe that a command of God authorizes us to disobey leaders? What would you do to verify such a belief?

**For Thought and Discussion:** Luke doesn't record any pleas for protection in 4:24-30. Why do you think the believers apparently didn't make any?

**Optional Application:** How can you apply the attitudes in 4:24-30 to your own prayer life?

**For Thought and Discussion:** Compare 4:29-30 to 5:12-16. Was the believers' prayer answered? In your judgment, would such a prayer be answered today? Why or why not?

**Optional Application:** Describe at least one way in which you could apply the apostles' example in your own dealings with authorities or unbelievers.

**For Further Study:** Add 4:1-31 to your outline. Show how it adds to the themes of Acts.

**For Thought and Discussion:** Observe how the public regarded the believers and why (5:12-16). Is this at all relevant to the Church today? How, or why not?

**For Thought and Discussion:** Why do you think the Sadducees responded to the miracles with "jealousy" (5:17, compare 5:28)? Do you have any similar tendency in you?

9. What attitudes, priorities, and feelings does the prayer in 4:24-30 reflect?

______________________

______________________

______________________

______________________

______________________

______________________

## Gamaliel's counsel (5:12-42)

***No one else dared join them*** (5:13). Word of Ananias' and Sapphira's deaths (5:1-11) had spread and discouraged uncommitted spectators.

***Guilty of this man's blood*** (5:28). The Sanhedrin had condemned Jesus to death for blasphemy. If He really was the Messiah, then they were guilty of condemning an innocent man, as the apostles kept saying (2:23, 3:13-15, 4:10-11).

10. Peter said that the apostles and the Holy Spirit were both witnesses to Jesus' crucifixion, resurrection, and exaltation (5:30-32). The apostles were testifying to these facts through preaching and miracles (5:12-16,21). How was the Holy Spirit witnessing to Jesus' identity?

______________________

______________________

______________________

______________________

______________________

______________________

______________________

***Gamaliel*** (5:34). The leader of the more moderate of the two schools of Pharisees. He was the most renowned rabbi of his day for both his learning and his piety. One of his students was Saul (Paul; see 22:3).

11. Dozens of movements and revolts had arisen and dissolved in the last few decades; what lesson did Gamaliel draw from his two examples (5:35-39)?

***Flogged*** (5:40). The lawful Jewish penalty was forty lashes (Deuteronomy 25:3), but the rabbis required this to be reduced by one (2 Corinthians 11:24) to prevent anyone from accidentally exceeding the limit. Although the Jewish law was more humane than the Roman, people did sometimes die from thirty-nine lashes with a whip, and even a healthy person was left in agony for days.

The Sanhedrin accepted Gamaliel's counsel to release the apostles, but the flogging was a severe warning against flouting the council's authority.

12. How did the apostles respond to their sufferings (5:41-42)?

**For Thought and Discussion:** What does question 10 tell you about your role and God's in witnessing about Jesus?

**Optional Application:** Explain in your own words what Peter says about Jesus in 5:31. How is He your Prince and Savior? How can you treat Him like this?

**For Thought and Discussion:** To whom does God give the Holy Spirit (5:29,32)? How is this relevant to us?

**For Thought and Discussion:** How has God acted to accomplish His ends in 1:1-5:42?

13. What lessons can we draw from 5:12-42 that are relevant to our lives?

14. Reread questions 5, 9, and 13, and the "Optional Applications" in this lesson. What one insight about Jesus or example set by the early believers would you like to apply during the next week or so?

15. What action can you take (including prayer) to take this insight to heart and put it into practice?

16. On pages 32-34, write what you learned from 4:1-31 and 5:12-42 about the topics on those pages.

17. List any questions you have about 4:1-31 or 5:12-42.

## For the group

**Warm-up.** Ask the group, "Has being a Christian ever gotten you into trouble? If so, what happened? How did you feel and respond to opposition?"

**Read aloud and summarize.**

**The Sanhedrin's first warning.** The main issues here are why the authorities objected to the gospel and how the apostles responded. For application, you can explore why people reject the gospel today and how you should respond. However, later lessons will give you chances to talk about this. Acts 4:1-22 and 5:12-42 specifically raise the question of what we should do when civil or pastoral authority contradicts God's commands. How do we know when we need to obey God rather than men? Can you think of some specific examples when Christians have done or are doing this?

If you plan to spend time on this topic, it would be a good idea to look at some of the cross-references in the margins. You can assign one passage to each group member ahead of time.

**The believers' prayer.** Here the issue is again response to opposition. What example do the believers set, and how can you follow it?

**Summarize.**

**Wrap-up.** It isn't necessary for everyone to concentrate on a different application every week. If someone still wants to focus on last week's application, don't oblige him or her to switch to a new one. It often takes more than a week or two for the Spirit to effect lasting change in someone. You might ask the group to come prepared to share how application is going at the beginning of your next meeting. Encourage anyone who wants to do so to talk with you privately about application before then.

**Worship.** Use 4:23-31 as a model for your own prayers together.

1. Marshall, page 98; Leon Morris, *The Gospel According to Saint Luke* (Grand Rapids, Michigan: William B. Eerdmans Publishing Company, 1974), page 68.
2. *The NIV Study Bible,* page 1650; Barclay, page 37.
3. *The NIV Study Bible,* page 1650.
4. Marshall, page 99.
5. *The NIV Study Bible,* page 1476; Paul Winter, "Pharisees and Sadducees," *Jesus in His Time,* edited by Hans Jurgen Schultz, translated by Brian Watchorn (Philadelphia: Fortress Press, 1971), pages 47-56.
6. Marshall, page 100.

LESSON SIX

# ACTS 2:42-47, 4:32-5:11, 6:1-7

## Community

Between the landmark events of the Jerusalem church's growth, Luke inserted bits of information about the church's inner life. Some of it is shocking, but Luke chose each detail to show us something important about that first body of believers. As you read 2:42-47, 4:32-5:11, and 6:1-7, think about how your church is like and unlike the one described here.

**For Further Study:** a. Using a concordance, do a word study on *sharing, participation, communion, partnership,* or *fellowship* in the New Testament.

b. Study the concept of fellowship in Philippians 1:3-8, 22-30; 2:1-30; 4:2-3,10-18.

### Fellowship (2:42-47)

***Apostles' teaching*** (2:42). Everything the apostles had learned from Jesus (Matthew 28:20), as well as the facts and meaning of His death, burial, and resurrection (Acts 2:23-24, 3:15, 4:10). That is, the facts of the gospel, the truths about the Father, Jesus, and the Spirit, and the implications for Christian life.

**For Thought and Discussion:** Why is it so crucial for us to nurture fellowship? (See, for example, 1 Corinthians 12:12-26, Philippians 2:1-11, Hebrews 10:23-25.)

***Fellowship*** (2:42). The Greek word *koinonia* had rich meaning: sharing, participation, communion, partnership. It could mean the sharing of goods as a family, partnership in a business or other enterprise, and shared religious or other experiences. It implied a degree of community, intimacy, and interdependence.[1]

***Breaking of bread*** (2:42). Here this phrase means the Lord's Supper, the commemoration of the

**For Thought and Discussion:** Should we devote ourselves to the apostles' teaching and prayer alone as well as together? If so, why and how? If not, why not? Support your view with Scripture.

**For Thought and Discussion:** How is fellowship more than just friendliness on Sundays or getting together midweek? What else does it include?

**For Thought and Discussion:** In what enterprise are Christians partners (Philippians 1:5)? How do you live in light of this fact?

**Optional Application:** How important to you are the apostles' teaching, fellowship, the breaking of bread, and prayer? Is any one of these less important to you than the others? If so, why? Talk with God about this.

Last Supper (Luke 22:14-23). In Acts 2:46, it means the sharing of ordinary meals as a sign of fellowship (Luke 24:30,35).[2]

---

1. How can we devote ourselves to "the apostles' teaching" today?

_______________________________________________

_______________________________________________

_______________________________________________

_______________________________________________

2. Why is it important to do this together? (*Optional:* See Romans 12:3-8, Ephesians 4:1-16, 2 Timothy 3:16-17.)

_______________________________________________

_______________________________________________

_______________________________________________

_______________________________________________

3. How can you devote yourself to "the fellowship"? How can you share and participate with other Christians as partners? Think of some specific ways.

_______________________________________________

_______________________________________________

_______________________________________________

_______________________________________________

4. Why is the Lord's Supper important (Luke 22:14-23; 1 Corinthians 10:16-17, 11:23-26)?

_______________________________________________

_______________________________________________

_______________________________________________

_______________________________________________

5. Why should you devote yourself to prayer with other Christians?

______________________________________

______________________________________

______________________________________

______________________________________

______________________________________

6. What other significant details of the early life of the Church do you observe in 2:42-47?

______________________________________

______________________________________

______________________________________

______________________________________

______________________________________

______________________________________

______________________________________

***In the temple courts*** (2:46). The earliest believers were still devout Jews, keeping the traditions and acknowledging the temple rites (3:1, 21:20-24). They did not fully realize how much Jesus' death and resurrection had overturned the old order of the temple sacrifices. The Temple was the familiar place for worship, prayer, and teaching, so the Jewish believers naturally gathered there. It was perhaps the only place with enough space for three thousand believers.

## True sharing (4:32-37)

Luke noted in 2:44-45 that the believers felt such unity that each spent his own possessions when others were in need. He expands on this theme in 4:32-5:11 with a positive and a negative example.

**For Thought and Discussion:** Besides their meetings in the Temple, the early believers met in their homes for prayer, fellowship, teaching, the Lord's Supper, and common meals (2:42,46). Why is eating together a support to fellowship?

**Optional Application:** Plan a home meeting with some Christians in which you share a meal, prayer, and other kinds of fellowship.

**For Thought and Discussion:** Why were the early believers "filled with awe" (2:43)? Are you filled with awe, and should you be? Why or why not?

**For Thought and Discussion:** How is your church or fellowship group like and unlike what Luke describes in 2:42-47 and 4:32-37? Are there any ways in which you would like it to change? Pray for your church, and ask God to show you anything that you can do for it.

**For Thought and Discussion:** a. In your judgment, should modern Christians all sell their property and give the proceeds to the Church? Why or why not? Should some of us do this? If so, how can we know? (For example, see Luke 12:32-34; 2 Corinthians 8:1-15, 9:1-15; 2 Thessalonians 3:6-15; 1 Timothy 5:3-16.)

b. Do you think the modern Church should take responsibility for caring for all Church members who cannot support themselves and whose family cannot support them? Why or why not? (Some of the above references may help you ground your view biblically. Has a change in culture changed the Body of Christ's obligations?)

**Optional Application:** How can you put into practice the principles you state in question 9? How can you encourage your church to do so?

7. Why did the believers sell their goods to support others who were in want (4:32)?

______________________________________

______________________________________

______________________________________

8. How was this generosity related to 4:33?

______________________________________

______________________________________

______________________________________

______________________________________

***At the apostles' feet*** (4:35,37; 5:2). This phrase "suggests some kind of legal transfer expressed in formal language," a trust for the community rather than a personal gift to the apostles.[3]

Acts 12:12 shows that not every Christian in Jerusalem sold all of his or her property.

9. These early believers expressed their oneness—their fellowship—by taking responsibility for each other's needs. To what extent do you believe this is a model we should follow? Explain why your view is consistent with Scripture and sensible. (*Optional:* See 2 Thessalonians 3:6-15, 1 Timothy 5:3-16, 1 John 3:16-18.)

______________________________________

______________________________________

______________________________________

______________________________________

______________________________________

______________________________________

______________________________________

*Joseph . . . called Barnabas* (4:36). Luke chooses him as a fine example of the attitudes of 4:32-35 so as laudably to introduce a character important later in the story (11:19-30, 13:1-15:41).

## False sharing (5:1-11)

10. Examine 5:1-4 carefully. Exactly what was Ananias's sin? (For instance, was it wrong in itself not to sell all his property and give it to the church?)

11. What do you think might have motivated him to do this?

12. What did God teach the early believers by striking Ananias and Sapphira dead (5:1-11)?

13. Is there a lesson here for us? If so, what is it?

**For Thought and Discussion:** From 4:32,34-37 and 5:4, does it seem that believers were required to give their possessions to the church and that private property was not acknowledged? Or, did believers continue to own goods privately while selling and sharing for others' needs? What evidence supports your conclusion?

**For Further Study:** Observe how Barnabas lived out his nickname in the rest of Acts (9:27; 11:22-25; 15:37-39). How can you act as a "son of encouragement" for other Christians?

**For Thought and Discussion:** What does this story show about the Holy Spirit?

**For Thought and Discussion:** Why do you think God doesn't continue to strike people dead who lie to Him?

**For Thought and Discussion:** a. What qualities did the apostles require in the chosen seven (6:3)? How is this significant for us?

b. How were the seven men appointed (6:3,6)? Is this a model for us? How, or why not?

---

***Church*** (5:11). Luke uses this word for the first time here. The Greek word *ekklesia* was used in the Septuagint to render the Hebrew word for "the assembly or congregation of God's people."[4] Gentiles used *ekklesia* to denote political and other assemblies. The other Septuagint word for the congregation of God's people—*synagoge*—was already being used for Jewish places of worship, so the early Christians chose *ekklesia* to name both the local congregation (8:1, 11:22, 13:1) and the universal Church (20:28).[5]

## The seven Hellenists (6:1-7)

This scene serves as a bridge between 1:1-5:42 and 6:8-8:40. It wraps up Luke's snapshots of life in the Jerusalem church with an example of internal problem solving, a practical working out of fellowship. At the same time, it introduces us to a group within the church that will be pivotal in 6:8-8:40—the Hellenists. In 6:1-7 we see those Hellenists emerge who will take the next step on the road to fulfilling the commission in 1:8.

***Grecian Jews . . . Hebraic Jews*** (6:1). The church was still entirely composed of Jews, but there were two somewhat distinct kinds of Jews in the Roman world. On the one hand were Hellenists or Grecian Jews; these spoke Greek as their primary language and displayed Greek customs and attitudes more than their Hebraic brethren. On the other hand were the Hebraists; these spoke Aramaic and/or Hebrew as their first language (though almost all could speak Greek as well), and they were more (though not entirely) resistant to Greek culture. There were devout, law-practicing Jews among both Hellenists and

Hebraists, although their customs differed. For the most part, Hebraists were natives of Palestine and Hellenists of other parts of the Roman Empire, but even this distinction was not absolute. The chief distinction was that Jerusalem had Hellenistic synagogues that worshiped in Greek and Hebraic ones that worshiped in Hebrew; Hebraists tended to consider Hellenists too liberal, and Hellenists regarded Hebraists as narrow-minded and self-satisfied.[6]

***Widows*** (6:1). Widows were vulnerable in the ancient world because wage work was seldom available for women, and women had fewer legal rights than men; women depended on male relatives for livelihood and protection. Elderly Jewish widows from all over the Empire often moved to Palestine to spend their last days. If they became destitute, the Jewish community may have supported some of them. There may have been a large number of Hellenistic widows who became the responsibility of the church rather than the synagogue when they became Christians.[7]

***Wait on tables*** (6:2). Behind this phrase lies the Greek word from which we get the word *deacon* (see the note on "ministry" on page 26). The Seven may not have been called deacons as a distinct office, but the Church eventually began to assign to deacons the function of caring for material needs.[8]

***They chose Stephen . . . Nicolas*** (6:5). All seven had Greek names and were probably Hellenists.[9]

***Prayed and laid their hands on them*** (6:6). "Laying on of hands was used in the Old Testament period to confer blessing (Genesis 48:13-20), to transfer guilt from sinner to sacrifice (Leviticus 1:4) and to commission a person for a new responsibility (Numbers 27:23). In the New Testament period, laying on of hands was observed in healing (Acts 28:8, Mark 1:41), blessing (Mark 10:16), ordaining or commissioning (Acts 6:6, 13:3; 1 Timothy 5:22) and imparting of spiritual gifts (Acts 8:17, 19:6; 1 Timothy 4:14; 2 Timothy 1:6)."[10]

**For Thought and Discussion:** What does laying on of hands signify today?

**For Thought and Discussion:** Why is it significant that many priests of the Jewish Temple became believers in Christ (6:7)? Keep this in mind as you study 6:8-8:3.

**For Thought and Discussion:** In what ways were the problem and its solution in 6:1-7 unique, and in what ways are they a model for us?

14. It's risky to decide that because something is done in Acts, we should do it today. However, does 6:1-7 have any lessons relevant to us?

15. From 2:42-47, 4:32-5:11, and 6:1-7, summarize the things that mattered to the early believers.

16. What one insight from 2:42-47, 4:32-5:11, or 6:1-7 would you like to apply to your life this week? (Perhaps you found something you want to help your church apply.)

17. What specific action can you take toward applying this insight?

18. Write any notes about the Church's mission, etc. on pages 32-34.

19. If you have any questions about 2:42-47, 4:32-5:11, or 6:1-7, list them here.

______________________________________

______________________________________

______________________________________

______________________________________

**For Further Study:**
**Add 2:42-47, 4:32-5:11, and 6:1-7 to your outline.**

## For the group

Instead of trying to deal with all the issues in this lesson, choose a few to focus on.

**Warm-up.** Discuss how your attempts to apply Acts have been going for the past five weeks. What opportunities have you had? How can the group be of help?

**Read aloud and summarize.**

**Fellowship.** One hard aspect of this lesson is not viewing the early Church through the lens of your own church's customs. Help the group to think about the early Church on its own terms, and then compare it to your modern church. (What did fellowship, the Lord's Supper, prayer, and the apostles' teaching mean to the first Christians? Then, how is your church similar and different? Should the emphases in your personal lives or your church's life change? If so, how and why?)

Your group is a perfect place to begin practicing devotion to fellowship, prayer, and the apostles' teaching. If you can't share the Lord's Supper, consider sharing a meal. Make some specific plans for *devoting* yourselves to fellowship. Think about all the meanings of *koinonia*—sharing (What can you share?), partnership (In what enterprise are you partners, and how can you act that way?), participation, and so on.

**True sharing.** Group members' political views may influence their perceptions of 4:32-37. Help the group examine the passage carefully—is it describing communism, or what? The church comprised only a few thousand people in Jerusalem; could a modern church take on the responsibility to care for all its poor members? Why or why not? What risks would this involve? Does God want us to take these risks, or does this early Church practice not apply to us?

**False sharing.** This story may raise such questions as: "Why did God strike the sinners dead? What does this say about Him?" It is a strange story to modern ears, but try to see why God might have done such things in the Church's infancy. Discuss what Ananias and Sapphira did wrong, and how you can avoid the same sin.

**The Seven.** Here we find the Church dealing with a problem brought on by growth and diversity. In what ways were the problem and its solution unique, and in what ways are they a model for us? (Should a church still set aside some members to care for widows and other needy members? What are some good ways of dealing with ethnic or other divisions in a church?)

**Summarize.**

**Worship.** Thank God for giving us stories about the early Church to be examples for us to follow. Ask for wisdom and discipline to apply these examples properly. Thank God for the apostles' teaching, the Lord's Supper, prayer, and fellowship. Ask for guidance in devoting yourselves to these.

1. Marshall, page 83; Jerry Bridges, *True Fellowship* (Colorado Springs: NavPress, 1985), page 17.
2. Marshall, page 83; *The NIV Study Bible,* page 1648.
3. Marshall, pages 109, 111.
4. Marshall, page 114.
5. Lothar Coenen, "Church, Synagogue" *The New International Dictionary of New Testament Theology,* volume 1, pages 291-305.
6. Carolyn Osiek, *What Are They Saying About the Social Setting of the New Testament* (Ramsey, New Jersey: Paulist Press, 1984), pages 11-23.
7. Fee and Stuart, page 94.
8. Marshall, page 126.
9. Marshall, page 127.
10. *The NIV Study Bible,* page 1654

LESSON SEVEN

# ACTS 6:8-8:3

## First Martyr

Through chapter 5, the spotlight was on the Aramaic-speaking Jewish Christians in Jerusalem: the apostles. Luke introduced the other segment of the church—Greek-speaking Jews—in 6:1-7, and foremost among them he named Stephen. The apostles, who faithfully attended temple services and followed the customs of Jewish tradition, were "highly regarded by the people" (5:13) even though the authorities detested them. But Stephen and his Hellenistic Christian brethren were arousing the ire of the other Jews in their synagogues. Observe the next stage of the drama in 6:8-8:3.

1. Review your outline of Acts or the ones on page 12. Does closer study suggest any ways you can improve your summary of 1:1-6:7? Recall what 6:8-9:31 is about, and consider how 6:8-8:3 fits into this section. Then read 6:8-8:3 at least once.

---

***Full of God's grace and power . . . wonders and miraculous signs*** (6:8). What was true of the apostles (4:33, 5:12) was also true of Stephen. (See 6:5, which was true even before the apostles laid their hands on Stephen.)

***Synagogue of the Freedmen*** (6:9). Freedmen were former slaves—prisoners of war or their descendants. For example, when the Roman general Pompey conquered Judea in 64 BC, he took many Jews prisoner to Rome who were later released.

Ten or more adult Jewish men could form their own synagogue for study of the Scriptures and worship. People preferred to join with others of like background in relatively small groups; mass meetings were for the Temple.

It's not clear if 6:9 speaks of one, two, three, or five synagogues. F. F. Bruce[1] thinks all four of the ethnic groups were freedmen meeting in one synagogue; I. H. Marshall[2] thinks the freedmen, Cyrenians, and Alexandrians were in one synagogue, while the Cilicians and Asians were in a second.

***Cyrene*** was the chief city in Libya and ***Alexandria*** the chief in Egypt (and the largest in the Empire after Rome)—both of these were in North Africa. ***Cilicia and Asia*** were two provinces in Asia Minor; Ephesus was the capital of Asia and Tarsus was a major town in Cilicia. (See the map on page 20.) One of the men of Cilicia who probably debated Stephen was Saul of Tarsus, a student of Rabbi Gamaliel (5:34, 9:11, 22:3).

***Blasphemy against Moses and against God*** (6:11). Specifically, 6:13-14 says they accused Stephen of speaking against the Temple (saying that Jesus would destroy it and end its sacrifices and rites) and against the Law (saying that the commands given to Moses need no longer be obeyed). The charges against Jesus were similar. Jesus prophesied that the Temple would be destroyed (Mark 13:2) and said that the Jews would destroy the temple of His body (John 2:18-21), so He was accused of promising to destroy and replace the Temple (Mark 14:57-59). Jesus also criticized not the Law of Moses but the Pharisees' and Sadducees' interpretations of that Law (Matthew 5:17-6:18, 12:1-14, 15:1-9, 19:1-12). Since the Jewish leaders considered their interpretations to be the same as the Law itself, they judged that Jesus spoke against God's Law.

***Covenant of circumcision*** (7:8). A covenant was a treaty or contract between two individuals; in this case, it was between a sovereign (the Lord) and His subject (Abraham). The Lord promised to be Abraham's God, protect him, give him heirs, and grant him and his heirs real estate in Palestine. In exchange, Abraham agreed to obey God and to show his commitment by circumcising every male in his household (Genesis 17:1-14). Cutting away the foreskin signified the dedication of "cutting a covenant" ("May I and my heirs be cut off if I do not remain loyal to God"; see Genesis 17:14). Metaphorically, circumcision symbolized cutting away "pride and sinfulness from the heart"[3] (Leviticus 26:41, Deuteronomy 10:16, Jeremiah 4:4, Acts 7:51). The covenant of circumcision predated both the Law and the Temple; Paul makes clear the implications of this in Romans 4.

***Angel*** (7:30,35,38,53). The book of Exodus does not say that God spoke through angels on either occasion at Mount Sinai, but the Jews of Stephen's day believed that He had done so.[4]

***Deliverer*** (7:35). The Greek word *lytrotes* comes from the verb "to redeem." In the New Testament, only Moses is called a redeemer, never Jesus, but Stephen's choice of this word (and others in 7:35-39) would have suggested to Christians a comparison between Moses and Jesus.[5]

***Living words*** (7:38). "Living oracles" in NASB. These are the Ten Commandments and the rest of the Law.

***Tabernacle*** (7:44). From Moses to David, Israel's sacrifices and rituals centered around the sacred tent whose pattern God had given Moses (Exodus 25:1-27:21). Its principal contents, the tablets inscribed with the Ten Commandments, was called ***the Testimony*** (Exodus 25:16,21).

---

2. The Hellenistic Jews accused Stephen of speaking against the Temple and the Law. Were these accusations true (6:11,13-14)? What does Luke say?

________________________________

________________________________

**For Thought and Discussion:** What did Stephen's comments about the tabernacle (7:44-47) have to do with his criticism of the Jewish attitude toward the Temple?

**Optional Application:** Do you idolize anything the way the Jews idolized their interpretation of the Law and their Temple? Pray about this.

3. Stephen answered the charges and gave his testimony in 7:2-53. What pattern in Jewish history did Stephen trace through Joseph (7:9-16), Moses (7:17-39), and Jesus (7:51-52)? What was similar about these men and their experiences with the Jews (see 7:9-10,25-29,35-39,51-52)?

4. What did Stephen imply was wrong with the Jews' attitude toward the Temple (7:48-50)?

5. The Jews thought their Temple in the Holy City was *the* holiest place on earth, the center of God's dealings with His people. How did Stephen's account of Israel's history subtly explode that myth? (See 7:2,9,30-34,36,38.)

6. Stephen also repeatedly mentioned God's promises to Abraham (7:2-8,17,32,34-37). How was God's promise relevant to Stephen's view of the Jewish laws?

7. Now that you've looked at Stephen's speech in some detail, answer the high priest's question (7:1). What were Stephen's beliefs about . . .

Moses and the Law (7:22,35-39,53)?

the Temple (7:41-50)?

8. Stephen did not just answer the charges against him; he responded with charges of his own (7:51-53). What were his accusations and assertions that roused the Jews to fury?

**For Thought and Discussion:** In both the Law of Moses (7:39-41) and the Prophets (7:42-43), the Jews were condemned for worshiping divinities in man-made idols (7:41). How was this fact relevant to the way the Jews treated the Temple (7:48)?

**For Thought and Discussion:** How were the Jews disobeying the Law (7:53)? See Acts 7:48,51-52 and Deuteronomy 5:4-11,17,20; 18:15-22.

**For Thought and Discussion:** From Luke 23:34,46 and Acts 7:59-60, what did Stephen apparently believe about Jesus and the Father?

***Glory of God*** (7:55). The glowing cloud that was the visible manifestation of God's presence and hid Him from view (Exodus 16:10, 24:17, 40:34-35).[6] Compare Acts 7:2.

***Son of Man*** (7:56). This was Jesus' favorite title for Himself, but rarely in the New Testament does anyone else call Him this. "In Daniel 7:13-14 the Son of Man is pictured as a heavenly figure who in the end times is entrusted by God with authority, glory and sovereign power."[7] Jesus often spoke of the Son of Man in connection with His rejection, death, resurrection, and exaltation to the right hand of God (Luke 9:22, 22:69). He also told His disciples that they must be willing to suffer for the Son of Man (Luke 9:23-26, 12:8-12). Thus, in his moment of acknowledging and suffering for Jesus, Stephen sees Him as the Son of Man ***standing*** (not sitting, as in Luke 22:69 and Acts 2:34) to welcome His first martyr into heaven.[8]

***Covered their ears . . . yelling*** (7:57). To block out the sound of blasphemy.

***Stone him*** (7:58). The Sanhedrin was not authorized to carry out executions; that was why they sent Jesus to the Roman governor. However, this was "a spontaneous act of mob violence"[9]—a lynch mob. The Romans looked the other way.

***Lord Jesus, receive my spirit . . . do not hold this sin against them*** (7:59-60). The prayers Jesus offered to the Father at His death (Luke 23:34,46) Stephen offered to Jesus.

---

9. Stephen's words in 7:55-56 moved his audience to riot and stone him for blasphemy (7:57-58). Why?

______________________________________

______________________________________

______________________________________

______________________________________

10. Stoning is an agonizing death. What is significant about Stephen's response to it (7:59-60)?

______________________________

______________________________

______________________________

______________________________

______________________________

______________________________

***Persecution*** (8:1). It was directed chiefly against the Hellenists, for the apostles were allowed to stay in Jerusalem. It probably died down after some weeks or months, for many disciples were able to return (9:26-29). However, it accomplished God's purpose.

11. How did the persecution of the Hellenistic Jewish Christians in Jerusalem serve the progress of the Church?

1:8; 8:1,4 ______________________________

______________________________

______________________________

7:58,60; 8:1,3; 9:1-6 ______________________________

______________________________

______________________________

12. What lessons for us does 6:8-8:3 offer?

sins of the Jews to avoid ______________________________

______________________________

______________________________

______________________________

______________________________

**Optional Application:** How do you feel about those who hate or hurt you? Can you follow Stephen's example? Ask God to help you.

**Optional Application:** Are you willing to risk persecution to proclaim and live the gospel? Pray about this.

**For Further Study:** Add 6:8-8:3 to your outline.

examples of Stephen to follow

key truths about God, Jesus, and the Spirit (6:8,10; 7:2-60)

13. What one of these lessons seems most relevant to you? What would you like to apply this week?

14. How can you respond in prayer and action to make this insight part of your life?

15. Write down any notes you have from 6:8-8:3 on the topics on pages 32-34.

**Study Skill—Obstacles to Application**

Here are some of the most frequent obstacles to applying God's Word:

1. "I didn't have time to meditate on and pray about a passage this week." Answer: What do you think about while in the car, getting dressed, or doing other things besides working and talking? Most people have at least a few minutes a day in which they can think about God rather than earthly concerns. Try turning off the radio and television, and just being quiet with God.

2. "I forget to think about Scripture during my free moments." Make reminders: tape a card with a reminder or quotation to your dashboard, refrigerator, desk, or mirror. Tie a string on your finger, purse, or briefcase. Try any gimmick that helps! It's important to let the Scripture come to mind frequently during the day.

3. "I can't ever think of specific ways to act on what the Scripture says." Divide your life into spheres (home, work, church, school . . .) or people (spouse, children, co-workers, boss, church friends . . .). Choose one person, and pray about what that person needs from you, what might prevent you from fulfilling that need, and how you might fulfill that need. Or, review a recent situation in which you sinned. Look for a similar situation in the near future to act rightly. Ask God to enable you to recognize and respond rightly to the situation.

Persistent prayer, inviting God to show you opportunities to apply what you have learned, will be answered.

16. Write down any questions you have about 6:8-8:3.

______________________________

______________________________

______________________________

______________________________

## For the group

**Warm-up.** Give everyone a chance to recount briefly any opportunities he or she had to proclaim the gospel or practice fellowship during the past week. You may be able to learn from each others' experiences.

**Read aloud and summarize.**

**Stephen's speech.** Stephen's speech may be difficult for those who aren't fully versed in Israel's history and Jewish attitudes toward the Law and the Temple. If needed, here is some help for questions 3-9: Stephen saw a pattern of men rejecting the Deliverer whom God had chosen. He observed that the Jews were treating the manmade Temple like the man-made idols (7:41,48). Against the Jews' pride in Jerusalem, he stressed God's activity in Ur, Egypt, and the "holy ground" of Sinai. Against their pride in the Law, Stephen discussed the promises to Abraham that predated that Law by over five hundred years.

Once you understand Stephen's message to the Jews, ask yourselves how it applies to you. Do you idolize anything? Do you take pride in God's Word but disobey it (7:53)? Do you try to box God into your traditions? Try to put yourselves into the Jews' place.

**Worship.** Thank God for filling His spokesmen with His Spirit. Thank Him for Abraham, Joseph, Moses, and Jesus—especially for the Son of Man who welcomes His witnesses into the Father's presence.

1. F. F. Bruce, *The Book of Acts* (Grand Rapids, Michigan: William B. Eerdmans Publishing Company, 1954), page 133.
2. Marshall, page 129.
3. Marshall, page 147.
4. Marshall, page 147.
5. Marshall, page 142.
6. Sverre Aalen, "Glory, Honor," *The New International Dictionary of New Testament Theology*, volume 2 (1976), pages 44-48.
7. *The NIV Study Bible*, page 1510.
8. Marshall, page 149.
9. Marshall, page 148.

LESSON EIGHT

# ACTS 8:4-40

## Philip's Journeys

The persecution of Hellenistic believers had at least one good effect: it got people like Philip out of Jerusalem and into the rest of Palestine. Acts 8:4-40 gives a few examples of what one man did in Samaria and Judea; Luke probably heard these stories when he visited Philip twenty-five years later (21:8). We shouldn't imagine that Philip was the only evangelist at work (8:4); he was simply the one with whom Luke was later able to speak.

As you read 8:4-40, consider how it fits into the overall plan of Acts and what it reveals about the Christian mission.

### The Samaritans (8:4-25)

***Philip*** (8:5). He was one of the Seven chosen from the Greek-speaking Jewish branch of the church in Jerusalem to manage the daily distribution (6:5). Saul's persecution focused on the Hellenists because Stephen had been one of their leaders.

***Samaria*** (8:5). There was a longstanding feud between Jews and Samaritans. When Solomon died back in 930 BC, his kingdom split in two: the northern tribes of Israel rejected the southern Judah. The northerners chose the city of Samaria as their capital, and they set up a temple and a cult to rival those in Jerusalem. The two nations were at war off and on until Assyria overran Israel in 723 BC, destroyed Samaria, and deported most of the Israelite population. Thereafter, the whole territory of Israel was known as Samaria.

The Assyrians settled pagans from other parts of their empire in Samaria. Some Samaritans remained loyal to the God of Israel, but most worshiped Him alongside other gods with mixed pagan and Israelite customs. The Samaritan version of the Law of Moses differed slightly from the Judan (Jewish) version, and as the centuries passed, Samaritan and Jewish approaches to the ancestral faith diverged more and more. The Samaritans built a temple on Mount Gerizim to rival the one in Jerusalem. Thus, Jews regarded Samaritans not as Gentiles but as heretics, a deplorable quasi-Jewish cult.[1] Some Samaritans were more godly than some Jews (Luke 10:33-37, 17:11-19), but Samaritans and Jews generally despised and avoided each other (Luke 9:52-56).

***The Christ*** (8:5). The Jews expected a Messiah who would be descended from King David and a powerful ruler like him. The Samaritans had rejected the Davidic kings in 930 BC, so they did not share the Jewish doctrines of the Messiah. Instead, they awaited the *ta'eb*, "the restorer"—a teacher, lawgiver, and deliverer like Moses (Deuteronomy 18:15-22, John 4:25).[2]

***Sent Peter and John*** (8:14). The Samaritan mission was an initiative of the Hellenists, but the apostles (the Hebraic leadership in Jerusalem) took responsibility to inspect and affirm new communities of believers. This was especially important when a radical new step like evangelizing Samaritans was taken (compare 11:22).

---

1. Questions 1 and 5 will help you compare the two episodes in 8:4-25 and 8:26-40.

   a. In 8:4-25, who is evangelized, convinced, and baptized?

   ______________________________

b. What do the Jews think of these people (John 4:9)?

c. How is this group's conversion significant to the progress of the gospel? (Recall who has been converted up to now.)

d. What convinces this group to become believers (8:6-8,12)?

e. What is the apostles' role in bringing this group into the Church (8:14-17)?

**For Further Study:** How does Acts 8:4-40 exemplify Ephesians 2:11-22?

**Study Skill—Patterns of Practice in Acts**

The apostles' role in 8:14-17 has created much confusion for later Christians. Romans 8:1-17 asserts that no one who does not have the Holy Spirit is a Christian. Hence, Acts 8:14-17 has just three explanations:

1. The Samaritans were not yet real believers. (But would Philip have baptized them if he had any doubt about their faith? Luke casts no doubt on either their faith or Philip's judgment in; the apostles added no teaching to what Philip had given.)

2. A person can receive the Spirit only when an apostle (or his successor?) lays hands on him.

3. God withheld the Spirit in this unique case so that the apostles could confirm that Samaritans were part of the Church.

Explanation (2) assumes that 8:14-17 is normative for all time, while explanation (3) states that the Samaritans' case differed from most others. We test these alternatives by *examining what happens elsewhere in Acts*. We find that:

a. In 19:1-7, the men at Ephesus have not yet been baptized into Jesus or received the Spirit; they receive both at once, with laying on of hands by an apostle.

b. In 10:44-48, the Spirit comes on people *before* baptism, without laying on of hands, and after only hearing the gospel.

c. In 2:38, the Spirit comes without laying on of hands but after hearing the gospel.

d. In 9:17, Saul receives the Spirit when Ananias, not an apostle, lays hands on him.

This variety suggests that neither the order "water baptism then Spirit reception" nor the order "apostolic laying on hands then Spirit reception" is a rule or norm. Instead, the experience varies according to what God wants to do in the particular situation. The principle illustrated is that *when Acts records variety, none of the patterns is probably a norm; when Acts records uniformity, the pattern is more probably a norm.* Baptism and Spirit reception are norms for Christians; the manner and order of these events are not.[3]

2. Why do you think it was important for God to use the apostles to demonstrate officially that Samaritans were true participants in the Church (John 4:9,21-24)? Why wasn't Philip's confirmation enough in this case?

_______________

_______________

_______________

_______________

_______________

---

***Simon*** (8:9). Another thread in 8:4-25 concerns Simon, a magician. The Roman world was full of men like this. Astrologers, prophets, philosophers, cult priests, and sorcerers traveled throughout the Empire offering their services to predict destiny, compound love potions, or influence the gods for money.[4]

After Luke's time, Simon was known as a dangerous opponent of Christianity and the father of the heresy called Gnosticism.[5]

***Great Power*** (8:10). Simon was being acclaimed to be either God, a god, or an emanation or representative of God.[6]

---

3. What was so terrible about Simon's request in 8:18-19?

_______________

_______________

_______________

_______________

4. Why do you think Luke recorded the episode with Simon? What does it add to the story of Acts?

_______________

**Optional Application:** Do people ever try to buy spiritual authority today? Think of one example, and examine your own life.

**For Thought and Discussion:** According to 8:18-24, is it possible for a baptized person to sin seriously and be forgiven? Why or why not?

______________________________________

______________________________________

______________________________________

______________________________________

## The Ethiopian eunuch (8:26-40)

***Desert road*** (8:26). This hot, nearly deserted route was a much less likely mission field than Samaria.[7]

***Ethiopian eunuch*** (8:27). He was from the country south of Egypt (modern Sudan, not modern Ethiopia). In those days, men were often castrated to serve as court officials. A eunuch could not have been a convert to Judaism because eunuchs were barred from the congregation (Deuteronomy 23:1). However, he could have been what the Jews called a "God-fearer," a Gentile who believed in the One True God, obeyed the moral laws of Judaism, and worshiped in the synagogue and the part of the Temple open to Gentiles.[8] (Compare Acts 10:2, 13:16, 16:14.)

***Candace*** (8:27). The title of the queen mother of ancient Ethiopia (like Pharaoh or Caesar). The king was considered too sacred for political and economic matters, so the queen was the effective ruler of the land.[9]

***Chariot*** (8:28). It was probably an ox-drawn wagon, slow enough for Philip to run beside easily.[10]

***Heard the man reading*** (8:30). In ancient times, people normally read aloud, not silently as we do.[11]

***Who is the prophet talking about . . . ?*** (8:34). The Jews were not certain on this point. Some said the Servant was Israel or a godly part of Israel (Isaiah 44:1-2); some said Isaiah referred to himself (as Jeremiah did in Jeremiah 11:18-20); some said he spoke of the Messiah of Isaiah 11 or the Son of Man of Daniel 7:13.[12]

5. Keep question 1 in mind as you answer these questions.

   a. Who accepted the gospel in 8:26-40?

   ______________________________

   b. What status did this kind of person have with the Jews (Deuteronomy 23:1)?

   ______________________________

   ______________________________

   ______________________________

   ______________________________

   c. How was this person's conversion significant to the progress of the gospel (Psalm 68:31, Isaiah 56:3-5, Ephesians 2:11-18)?

   ______________________________

   ______________________________

   ______________________________

   ______________________________

   d. What was the apostles' role in taking the step to permit such a person into the Church? Why is this important?

   ______________________________

   ______________________________

   ______________________________

   ______________________________

   e. What convinced this person to be baptized (8:35)?

   ______________________________

   ______________________________

   ______________________________

   ______________________________

**For Thought and Discussion:** Did the eunuch need the laying on of hands to receive the Spirit? What evidence do we have (8:36-39)?

**For Thought and Discussion:** What good news (8:35) do you think Philip told the eunuch that made him want to be baptized? Explain from earlier speeches in Acts and/or from Isaiah 52:13-53:12.

**For Thought and Discussion:** Why do you think Luke makes a point of God's guidance in having the eunuch evangelized (8:26,29,39) but mentions no such guidance regarding the Samaritans? Why is God's guidance so important in the eunuch's case? (Consider Deuteronomy 23:1, Isaiah 56:3-5.)

**Optional Application:** Do you know anyone in a position like the Samaritans (8:5-12) or the eunuch (8:30-34)? How can you help that person?

6. Summarize what 8:4-40 contributes to the overall message of Acts.

7. How is this section relevant to your life? What sins to avoid, examples to follow, or truths about God does it offer?

8. What one insight from 8:4-40 would you like to apply? How can you do this?

9. Jot any notes on the topics on pages 32-34.

10. List any questions you have about 8:4-40.

**For Further Study:** Add 8:4-40 to your outline.

**For Thought and Discussion:** Why do you think Luke doesn't tell us whether Philip laid hands on the eunuch, whether he received the Spirit, or whether the Samaritans were immersed in water or had water poured over them?

**Study Skill—Norms from Acts**

Acts 8:36-39 makes it fairly clear that the eunuch was baptized by immersion in a pool or stream. However, we are fairly sure that there was no body of water in Samaria deep enough to immerse the Samaritans,[13] and Luke didn't bother to tell us what Philip did to them. Paul's language about baptism as burial (Romans 6:1-3) suggests that he presupposed immersion, but the early Christian manual called the *Didache* (written around 100 AD) says that if there is no cold, running water or warm, still water available for immersion, people may have water poured over them.[14] Thus, in the *Didache* immersion is the norm but pouring is an acceptable option, and in Scripture immersion is implied as the norm but often no one is concerned to specify. This suggests a question: *When the biblical narrative is not explicit about method, must we conform to a norm or are alternatives acceptable?*

# For the group

**Warm-up.** Ask, "What opportunities have you had to share the gospel this week? Has anything kept you from seizing all the chances you have had? If so, what has done so?"

**The Samaritans and the eunuch.** Compare your answers to questions 1 and 5. What similarities and differences do you find between the two situations?

Next, tackle the question of why the Samaritans needed the apostles' hands to receive the Spirit. Which explanation do you agree with, and why? Do you agree with the reasoning in the Study Skills on page 88 and above? Why or why not? (These are controversial topics. Be prepared for an argument over methods of baptism or the necessity of apostolic laying on of hands. If the Study Skills don't help you deal with these issues, go on to something else. Do you think God intended his book to decide these issues? Why or why not?)

If matters of church practice become divisive, focus on the primary matters Luke means to raise in 8:4-40: the spread of the gospel to people formerly outside the covenant. Why is this important to you? How can you imitate Philip and avoid imitating Simon?

**Summarize.**

**Evaluation.** This might be a good time to evaluate how your study is going. You might look back at the goals you set for your group in lesson one, and see if you want to change anything you are doing. Or, ask each person to tell what he or she likes best and least about this meeting or your meetings in general. Is anyone frustrated, bored, or confused about anything? If anyone is less than excited about the group, see what you can do about it together or privately.

**Worship.** Thank God for directing and enabling evangelists like Philip. Praise Him for spreading the gospel to improbable, rejected people (like Samaritans and foreign eunuchs) today.

1. An analogy might be that Moslems are plainly not Christians, but Mormons claim to be Christians although Christians dispute that claim.
2. Marshall, page 154.
3. Fee and Stuart, pages 94-102; Marshall, pages 157-158. See also Kent, pages 78-80.
4. John Ferguson, *The Religions of the Roman Empire* (Ithaca, New York: Cornell University Press, 1970), pages 179-189; Helmut Koester, *Introduction to the New Testament: Volume 1: History, Culture and Religion of the Hellenistic Age* (Philadelphia: Fortress Press, 1982), pages 376-381.
5. Marshall, pages 155, 159-160.
6. Marshall, page 155; John Rutherfurd, "Simon Magus," *The International Standard Bible Encyclopaedia*, volume 4, pages 2795-2797.
7. Marshall, pages 161-162.
8. Kent, page 81; Marshall, page 162; F. F. Bruce, *New Testament History* (Garden City, New York: Doubleday and Company, 1975), pages 145-147, 266. The word *eunuch* was occasionally used for a non-castrated official, but in a religious context Luke's readers would have probably assumed he meant the word literally.
9. *The NIV Study Bible,* page 1659; Marshall, page 162.
10. Marshall, page 162.
11. *The NIV Study Bible,* page 1659; Marshall, pages 162-163.
12. Marshall, pages 163-164; *The NIV Study Bible*, page 1659.
13. Fee and Stuart, page 100.
14. *The Didache* in *Early Christian Writings*, translated by Maxwell Staniforth (New York: Penguin Books, 1968), page 231; Fee and Stuart, page 100.

LESSON NINE

# ACTS 9:1-31, 11:19-30

## Saul Appointed

Philip disappears from the stage of Acts except for a walk-on twenty-five years later (21:8). Luke's camera shifts back to the young Pharisee Saul, whom we left in 8:3 arresting Christians on a house-to-house search. One of the momentous events in Church history is about to happen.

As you read 9:1-31 and 11:19-30, try to put yourself in Paul's, Ananias', the Jews', and the Jerusalem believers' places. Ask God to help you identify with these people.

### Saul's conversion (9:1-31)

***Letters*** (9:2). The Sanhedrin's authority over synagogues outside Judea probably didn't extend to arresting Jews in Damascus accused of blasphemy.[1] At this point in history, the Jewish communities were relatively independent. Instead, the Sanhedrin probably authorized Saul "to injure and even kidnap leading Christians, *if he could with impunity.*"[2]

***Damascus*** (9:2). An important city in the province of Syria because "it was the hub of a vast commercial network with far-flung lines of caravan trade reaching into north Syria, Mesopotamia, Anatolia, Persia and Arabia. If the new 'Way' of Christianity flourished in Damascus, it would quickly reach all these places."[3] Damascus was

**For Thought and Discussion:** Have you ever suddenly realized that your whole way of dealing with God was wrong? If so, how did you feel? What did you do?

**Optional Application:** What differences does Jesus' identity make to you?

**Optional Application:** How is your mission like and unlike Saul's? How are you fulfilling this mission, and how can you do so better?

about 150 miles (six days' journey) from Jerusalem.

***The Way*** (9:2). Believers apparently called their movement this. It referred to "the way to be saved" (16:17) or "the way of the Lord/God" (18:25-26); that is, *the* only way of life that God established by which people could be saved.[4]

***Did not eat or drink*** (9:9). For three days the blind Saul fasted in shock and penitence, as the dreadful realization of what God thought of his life began to dawn on him.[5]

***Saints*** (9:13,32). "Holy ones" or "persons set apart for God." The believers also called themselves ***all who call on your name*** (Acts 9:14) from the passage Peter quotes in Acts 2:21.

***After many days . . . a basket*** (Acts 9:23-25). Saul spent a brief time in Damascus, then went into the neighboring kingdom of Arabia. While he was there, his preaching evidently aroused the ire of Aretas IV, king of the Nabatean Arabs, so Saul returned to Damascus. Both Aretas's governor and the Damascene Jews wanted to kill Saul, so he had to escape the city in a basket (2 Corinthians 11:30-33, Galatians 1:13-18).[6]

---

In Acts 22 and 26, Saul/Paul retells the story of his conversion in speeches to the residents of Jerusalem and to King Agrippa. Since Paul adds details there that Luke omits in chapter 9, we'll look at parts of the later retellings here.

1. The episode on the Damascus road was a profound learning experience for Saul. What did he learn about . .

   who Jesus is (9:4-5,20,22; 22:14)?

   ______________________________

   ______________________________

   ______________________________

   ______________________________

what his own mission was going to be (9:15-16, 20-30; 22:14-16; 26:16-18)?

2. How else did his encounter with Jesus affect Saul?

9:8-9

9:1-2,20-30

3. Saul later emphasized that he saw Jesus Himself, not just a vision of Him (Acts 9:27, 22:14-15, 26:16; 1 Corinthians 9:1, 15:7-10). What did this mean for him (1 Corinthians 9:1)?

4. What roles did Stephen, Ananias, and Barnabas have in Saul's reconciliation with God and His people?

Stephen (Acts 7:60-8:1)

**For Thought and Discussion:** a. What was ironic about the way Saul entered Damascus (9:6,8)? How had he intended to enter the city (9:2)?

b. What lesson does this example offer us?

**Optional Application:** Has committing yourself to Christ changed your outlook and way of life as radically as Saul's were changed? (See Philippians 3:2-11.) Why or why not? What would your life be like if you took Saul's attitude?

**Optional Application:** a. How would you have felt in Ananias' place (9:10-16)? Would you have been comfortable calling Saul "Brother Saul" (9:17)? What does this show about Ananias?

b. In your opinion, were the Jerusalem disciples' feelings understandable (9:26)? Why or why not? What does 9:27 show about Barnabas (compare 4:36)?

Ananias (9:10-17)

Barnabas (9:26-27)

5. How do these men's examples apply to us?

6. Why is it important for us to think about the early Christians' willingness to suffer for Jesus' name (5:40-42; 7:59-60; 9:15-16,23-30)?

7. Like 6:7, 9:31 is a summary or progress report. Review your title for 6:8-9:31 (page 12 or your separate outline), and write an improved summary of this section if necessary. What does 6:8-9:31 add to the story of Acts?

______________________________

______________________________

______________________________

______________________________

______________________________

**Optional Application:** How can you join with other Christians in doing for someone what Stephen, Ananias, or Barnabas did for Saul?

**For Further Study:** Add 9:1-31 to your outline of Acts.

**For Thought and Discussion:** a. How do modern Christians suffer for Jesus' name?

b. How else is 9:1-30 relevant to Christians today?

***Tarsus*** (9:30, 11:25). Saul's birthplace (22:3). He was born a citizen of that city as well as of Rome (21:39, 22:25-29), so his family probably owned property or a business. (Only people with rank and/or property were citizens in their provincial towns, and Roman citizenship was even harder for non-Italians to obtain.) Tarsus was a prosperous city on the trade route from Syria to Ephesus. It was known for its schools of philosophy and liberal arts. If Saul's family were Greek-speaking Jews, he may have had some contact with Gentile schools. However, "Hebrew of Hebrews" in Philippians 3:5 may mean that Saul's people were Hebraists and kept away from Gentiles.[7] Also, it's possible that Saul moved to Jerusalem at a young age (22:3).

## The church in Antioch (11:19-30)

After recording Saul's departure for Tarsus, Luke reported some groundbreaking deeds of Peter (9:32-11:18), then returned briefly to Saul and Barnabas (11:19-30), then finished with Peter and the Jerusalem church (12:1-24), and finally focused on Saul and Barnabas (12:25-15:41). Luke had his reasons for alternating back and forth like this, but we will look at 11:19-30 now and deal with all the material about Peter in lesson ten. Acts 11:19 refers back to 8:1 again; as Philip went to Samaria and then Caesarea when the persecution started.

***Phoenicia*** (11:19). Modern Lebanon. ***Cyprus*** was an island in the Mediterranean and the home of Barnabas (4:36). See the map on page 20.

***Antioch*** (11:19). This is the Antioch in Syria, as opposed to the one in Pisidia (13:14). With about 500,000 people it was the third largest city in the Empire, after Rome and Alexandria. Because it was near the border between the Roman world and the Orient, Antioch had a cosmopolitan population. That included a large Jewish community which had attracted a particularly large number of converts from paganism (recall Nicolas from 6:5).[8] The city was a splendid example of Greek and Roman city planning, and a center for trade, tourism, and culture. Some of the chief attractions were the chariot races and the temple of Daphne.

According to the myth, Daphne was a woman whom Apollo pursued and whom Artemis changed into a laurel tree to protect her virginity. At night, the temple priestesses and worshipers reenacted the myth in sacred laurel groves; the priestesses were renowned cult prostitutes. "The morals of Daphne" was Greek slang for loose living.[9]

***Greeks*** (11:20). The term meant people who spoke Greek. The context suggests that Luke did not mean Greek-speaking Jews (Hellenists), since there was nothing new about evangelizing them. Rather, the Hellenistic Jewish believers from Cyprus and Cyrene were evangelizing Greek-speaking Gentiles—Syrians, Mesopotamians, Cappadocians, Romans, Greeks, and whatever other nationalities were represented in Antioch.

The first contact was probably with Gentile "God-fearers" in the synagogues, since if the Antiochene Jews had attracted many converts they had probably attracted many more sympathizers. Gentiles were often drawn to the Jewish God but repelled by circumcision and the food laws; these were a ripe harvest field for the followers of Jesus. There seems to have been no suggestion that the Gentile believers keep the Jewish laws until Judean believers arrived to insist on it (15:1).[10]

***They sent Barnabas*** (11:22). Nearly every cult known in the Empire was represented in Antioch, and it was common for people to participate in as many as they liked. Religions borrowed deities, doctrines, and rituals from each other, so there was no telling what Antiochene Gentiles might do to the gospel when they got hold of it. The apostles were therefore wise to send Barnabas to inspect the situation.

**Optional Application:** Imagine going back to your hometown to spread the gospel, as Paul probably did (9:30, 11:25). How would you feel?

***Saul*** (11:25). He had presumably been preaching in his hometown of Tarsus since he left Jerusalem about nine years earlier (9:30).[11]

***Christians*** (11:26). Latin for "those of the party of Christ," as "Herodians" means "those of the party of Herod" (Matthew 22:16). To the Jews, "Christ" was a sacred title—the Messiah—so they would never have used it in a nickname. The Gentile Antiochenes probably thought *Christos* was someone's name. "Christians" seems to have been what outsiders called the group; they called themselves "believers," "brethren," "those of the Way," or "disciples." "Christian" rarely occurs in the New Testament, and only in a possible context of ridicule (Acts 26:28, 1 Peter 4:16).[12]

***Prophets*** (11:27). Almost from the beginning of the Church, there seems to have been a recognized office of prophet, just as of apostle (1 Corinthians 12:28). Essentially, a prophet was someone inspired by the Holy Spirit to speak on God's behalf. Prophets exhorted, encouraged, explained how the Old Testament prophecies applied in the present, spoke God's current word to the community on contemporary matters, and foretold the future when God wanted the believers to act in preparation (Acts 13:1, 15:32, 19:6, 21:9-11; 1 Corinthians 14:3-5,24-33).[13]

***Famine*** (11:28). There were no recorded famines that devastated the entire Roman world, but the Roman historian Suetonius wrote that there were "frequent famines" in various parts of the Empire. There was definitely a famine in Judea in 46 AD, and since 47-48 AD was a Sabbath year when Jews were not permitted to cultivate the

**For Thought and Discussion:** a. What does question 9 tell you about Christian fellowship/partnership/sharing?

b. Is there any lesson here for you or your church?

land (Leviticus 25:1-7), the situation would have been serious. Agabus may have been prophesying this famine years ahead of the event.[14] ***Claudius*** was emperor from 41 to 54 AD.

---

8. What was the relationship between the churches in Jerusalem and Antioch (11:22,27-29)?

9. What laudable traits do Barnabas and the Christians at Antioch show in 11:19-30?

10. Look back at your answers to questions 1-9. What one insight from 9:1-31 and 11:19-30 would you like to apply to your life? How will you apply it?

11. Jot any notes from 9:1-31 or 11:19-30 on pages 32-34.

12. List any questions you have about these passages.

______________________________________________

______________________________________________

______________________________________________

______________________________________________

______________________________________________

**Optional Application:** How can you imitate one or more of Barnabas's traits?

**For Thought and Discussion:** What was the Holy Spirit's role in the events of 9:1-31 and 11:19-30? (Look carefully at the text.) How are your observations relevant to your life?

## For the group

**Warm-up.** Ask, "How did you feel the first time you realized that Jesus was God?" For some people, this is a joyful discovery; for others, like Saul, it is a terrible shock. Still others can't remember the first time, and they shouldn't feel guilty about this.

**Read aloud.**

**Summarize.** Summarize 9:1-31 and 11:19-30, then summarize 6:8-9:31.

**Saul's conversion.** Help the group identify with Saul. Recall why he persecuted the church (6:8-8:3), and discuss why he stopped, how he felt, and how he was changed. How were or are you like Saul either before or after conversion? How were or are you different? How would you like to follow Saul's example?

Try to identify with Ananias and Barnabas also.

**The church in Antioch.** Some in your group may want to discuss whether there are prophets in the church today. You may want to research the reasons why some Christians say "yes, in the full New Testament sense"; some say "yes, but they only proclaim God's Word and can't foretell the future"; and some say "no, there are no prophets in any sense." Or, you may prefer to direct interested people to a book rather than taking time in the discussion.

The central issue here is the spread of the gospel to Gentiles, but you'll discuss that in lesson ten.

Instead, you might use 11:19-30 as a springboard for discussing fellowship between churches. Remember that the believers in Antioch had a very different view of Christian lifestyle from the believers in Jerusalem, but only later did this contrast produce friction.

**Application.** This is a shorter lesson than some, so you may be able to take some extended time to share how your applications are going. Avoid making anyone feel guilty for not being like Peter or Stephen after just a few weeks. Instead, look for ways to help each other and apply together. What specific issues are you wrestling with?

**Summarize.**

**Worship.** Thank Jesus for what He revealed to Saul. Praise Him as the Christ, the Son of God, the Holy and Righteous One. Ask Him to make His personality and desires known to you as vividly as He did to Saul.

1. Marshall, page 168.
2. R. P. C. Hanson, *The Acts* (Oxford: Oxford University Press, 1967), page 112.
3. *The NIV Study Bible,* page 1661.
4. Marshall, page 168.
5. Marshall, page 170.
6. Marshall, page 174.
7. F. F. Bruce, *Paul: Apostle of the Heart Set Free* (Grand Rapids, Michigan: William B. Eerdmans Publishing Company, 1977), pages 32-43.
8. Flavius Josephus, *The Jewish War,* translated by H. St. James Thackeray, in The Loeb Classical Library (Cambridge: Harvard University Press, 1928, 1957), book 7, chapter 45; Marshall, page 201; Bruce, *Paul,* pages 130-133.
9. Barclay, page 89.
10. Marshall, pages 201-202.
11. Barclay, page 90. Bruce, *Paul,* pages 133 and 475, says that Paul was converted in about 33 AD, went to Tarsus in late 35 AD, and went to Antioch about 45 AD.
12. Marshall, page 203; Kent, page 99.
13. Gerhard Friedrich, "Prophetes," *Theological Dictionary of the New Testament,* page 963; *The NIV Study Bible,* pages 1667, 1750, 1754; Marshall, page 203.
14. Marshall, page 204; E. Lohse, "Sabbaton," *Theological Dictionary of the New Testament,* page 990.

LESSON TEN

# ACTS 9:32-11:18

## Peter Moves Out

The conversion of an Ethiopian Gentile (8:26-40) did not affect the policy of the Church because he returned immediately to his homeland and had no more contact with Jewish believers. However, two almost simultaneous events confronted the Jewish church with the issue of the Gentiles' place in their fellowship. One was the evangelism of Hellenistic Christians in Antioch (11:19-30). The other bore the authority of Peter himself, a leader of the Hebrew church in Jerusalem.

Read 9:32-11:18, trying to see the episodes from Peter's point of view.

**For Thought and Discussion:** Compare Acts 9:32-43 to Luke 4:18-19,38-39; 8:40-42,51-56. Why do you think it is important for us to know that Peter healed the sick and raised the dead (John 14:12-14)? (That is, why does Luke keep telling us these miracle stories?)

### Aeneas and Dorcas (9:32-43)

***Lydda*** (9:32). See the map on page 20. Lydda was a small town just north of the road from Jerusalem to ***Joppa*** (9:36). Joppa (modern Jaffa, near Tel Aviv) was the main seaport of Judea, some thiry-eight miles from Jerusalem and twelve miles from Lydda.[1] ***Sharon*** (9:35) was the coastal plain that ran fifty miles from Lydda and Joppa to Caesarea. (There is some evidence of a town named Sharon near Lydda.[2])

***Tanner*** (9:43). Common people often used their occupations as a kind of last name, but Simon's is significant. A man who tanned animal skins routinely touched dead creatures and so was ritually unclean according to Jewish law (Leviticus 11:39-40). Since anyone or anything he touched became unclean, a tanner was often despised by strict Jews. Also, the chemicals used in tanning smelled foul. Apparently, Peter was already beginning to overcome ingrained Jewish prejudices.[3]

## The conversion of Cornelius (10:1-11:18)

***Caesarea*** (10:1). Herod the Great built this harbor city in the Greek style shortly before the birth of Jesus, and it became the headquarters for the Roman administration. From 6-41 AD, a Roman *procurator* (Pontius Pilate was one of them) lived in Caesarea, and his troops were garrisoned there.[4]

Caesarea was thirty miles from Joppa, so it would have taken a full day on horseback for each leg of the journey.

***Centurion*** (10:1). The commander of a *century*, about a hundred soldiers. There were six centuries in a *cohort* and ten cohorts in a *legion*. Thus, Cornelius was roughly equivalent to a sergeant major or a captain over a company. Commanders of legions and cohorts were generally aristocrats who served for a year or two on their ways to high civilian office, but centurions were career military men chosen for their talent and character. They provided the stability that made the Roman army strong.[5]

***Italian Regiment*** (10:1). Literally, "the Italian Cohort" (RSV). These six hundred men were originally recruited from Italy.[6]

***God-fearing*** (10:2). A *proselyte* was someone who fully converted from paganism to Judaism; if he was a man, he underwent circumcision and kept the whole Jewish law. A *God-fearer* was a Gentile who was not circumcised and perhaps continued to eat Gentile food, but who attended and supported the synagogue, kept the moral laws, and prayed to the God of Israel. Acts 10:2 emphasizes Cornelius' sincere devotion.

***Three in the afternoon*** (10:3). Cornelius the God-fearer was observing a regular hour for Jewish prayer (3:1).

***Memorial offering*** (10:4). In God's ears, Cornelius' prayers were like one of the kinds of sacrifice in the Jerusalem Temple.

***Lord*** (10:4). Cornelius did not necessarily think the angel was God. "Lord" in those days was the polite address, equivalent to "Sir."[7]

***Roof to pray*** (10:9). A Middle Eastern house normally had a flat roof with an outside stairway. There was often a cloth awning over the roof to shield the sun. The inside of the house was hot, stuffy, smelly, and busy during the day, but the roof was cool and private for prayer or relaxation.[8]

***Animals . . . reptiles . . . birds*** (10:12). The three Old Testament categories of animals (Genesis 6:20, Romans 1:23). Leviticus 11:1-47 stated which creatures from each category were clean or unclean for food, and Jews were raised to consider unclean meat (including pork, shellfish, rabbit, and reptile) disgusting.

***Invited the men*** (10:23). Giving hospitality to Gentiles according to Jewish customs did not break Jewish law, since the food would be kosher. However, a deep-seated aversion often kept strict Jews from associating comfortably with Gentiles.

***Peter entered the house*** (10:25). It was a "distinct breach of custom"[9] for a Jew even to enter a Gentile's house, since everything in it was unclean by contact with unclean Gentiles.

***I am only a man*** (10:26). People often knelt before their superiors in the cultures of both the Old Testament and the Roman Empire. However, Christians disavowed such reverence because it was similar to the honor given a god. When there was a possibility of misunderstanding, Peter and others made their position clear (Acts 14:14-15; Revelation 19:10, 22:9).[10]

**For Further Study:** Compare Acts 10:1-48 to Luke 7:1-10.

**Optional Application:** In what ways is Cornelius a model for us? Specifically how can you apply that model to your priorities and actions?

1. What was the immediate lesson of Peter's trance vision in 10:9-16?

2. After the messengers from Cornelius came and reported the angelic appearance, what further application of the vision was apparent to Peter (10:23-29)?

3. When Peter observed Cornelius' manner and heard his account of the angel's message, what did Peter realize (10:34-35)?

4. In what sense does God "not show favoritism" (10:34)? From this story, what kinds of things don't influence God to love a person?

5. Peter said God was willing to accept all those "who fear him and do what is right" (10:35). Did this mean that Cornelius' good deeds had earned him salvation? Why or why not, in light of the whole context of the story (especially 10:22,33,43-48)?

________________________________________

________________________________________

________________________________________

________________________________________

________________________________________

________________________________________

________________________________________

________________________________________

6. Peter's speech to this Gentile household differed in several ways from what he said to Jewish audiences. What key points did he make in this instance (10:36-43)?

________________________________________

________________________________________

________________________________________

________________________________________

________________________________________

________________________________________

________________________________________

________________________________________

________________________________________

***Peace*** (10:36). Reconciliation between God and man, and all the blessings that proceed from that reconciliation: wholeness in relationships, security, inner tranquility, etc.[11]

**For Thought and Discussion:** How did Cornelius show that he feared God and did what was right (10:35; see also 10:1-8,30-33)?

**Optional Application:** Why is it important for you that God doesn't show favoritism? Do you ever act as though He does favor certain ethnic, economic, social, or political groups?

**For Thought and Discussion:** If Cornelius already feared God and did right, then why did he need Jesus?

**For Thought and Discussion:** How is 10:34-43 a model for a way you can explain the gospel to people you encounter?

**For Thought and Discussion:** Why was each aspect of Peter's sermon important for the Gentiles to grasp if they were to have a good understanding of Jesus? (Also, how is each aspect important to you?)

**For Thought and Discussion:** Why are doing good and healing the demonized notable aspects of Jesus' work (10:38)? To what extent do you believe they are part of your work? Why do you think this?

**For Thought and Discussion:** What would you say to someone who asked why the resurrected Jesus appeared only to certain witnesses, not the crowds (10:41)?

**For Thought and Discussion:** Why was it necessary to baptize the Gentiles in water in addition to their experience in 10:44-46? (*Optional:* see Matthew 28:19.)

***What has happened throughout Judea*** (10:37). Like the Gospel of Mark, Peter began with the ministry of John the Baptist, covered Jesus' ministry, and culminated with Jesus' resurrection appearances. Around 140 AD, the Christian writer Papias recorded that Mark was a "close associate of Peter" and that his Gospel was a collected account of Peter's testimony about Jesus.[12]

Peter's speeches to the Jews did not mention Jesus' earthly ministry as much as the Jews' rejection.

---

7. What unprecedented thing happened in the middle of Peter's speech (10:44-46)?

______________________________

______________________________

______________________________

8. What did this signify?

______________________________

______________________________

______________________________

______________________________

9. Why were Peter's fellow Jewish believers astonished (10:45)?

______________________________

______________________________

______________________________

______________________________

10. What shocked the Jerusalem church most about the rumors from Caesarea was not that Peter had baptized Gentiles. What shocked them most, and why (11:1-3)?

______________________________

11. Consider Peter's account of the events (11:4-17). What was the significance of this whole episode (11:18), and why was it so important? (*Optional:* See Ephesians 2:11-22.)

12. It may be hard to imagine a time when the idea of a Gentile Christian was astonishing. Still, what is the most important insight about God, the gospel, the Church, or yourself that you have had from 9:32-11:18?

13. What would you like to do or pray about this truth? How do you want it to affect your life?

14. On pages 32-34, note what you learned from 9:32-11:18 about the Church's mission and message, fellowship, and the Holy Spirit.

**For Thought and Discussion:** Why did God need to use such extraordinary means as a trance and a vivid outpouring of the Spirit to get across the message of 10:34-35 and 11:18?

**For Further Study:** Add 9:32-11:30 to your outline. Divide the section however you think best.

15. List any questions you have about this passage.

______________________________

______________________________

______________________________

______________________________

## For the group

**Warm-up.** Ask the group, "Do you associate comfortably and frequently with nonChristians or Christians from very different denominations? Why or why not?"

**Aeneas and Dorcas.** Since you discussed Peter's gift of healing earlier, you may want to touch only lightly on this passage.

**Cornelius.** Help the group understand why evangelism and even association with Gentiles was so daring and hard for Jews like Peter. How can each of you practice the lesson that God taught Peter?

**Worship.** Thank God for not showing favoritism, for overcoming barriers between people, and for the Holy Spirit, who is the evidence of your acceptance by God.

1. Marshall, pages 178-179; *The NIV Study Bible,* page 1662.
2. *The NIV Study Bible,* page 1662.
3. D.J. Wiseman, "Arts and Crafts," *The New Bible Dictionary,* edited by J. D. Douglas (Grand Rapids, Michigan: Tyndale House, 1982), page 92.
4. Marshall, page 183; Bruce, *New Testament History,* pages 32-38.
5. Marshall, page 183; Barclay, page 79; James L. Jones, "The Roman Army," *Catacombs and the Colosseum,* edited by Stephen Benko and John J. O'Rourke (Valley Forge, Pennsylvania: Judson Press, 1971), pages 193-194, 201-203.
6. Marshall, page 183; *The NIV Study Bible,* page 1662.
7. Marshall, page 185.
8. *The NIV Study Bible,* page 1663.
9. Kent, page 93.
10. Marshall, page 188.
11. Hartmut Beck and Colin Brown, "Peace," *The New International Dictionary of New Testament Theology,* volume 2, pages 776-783.
12. *The NIV Study Bible,* page 1490.

LESSON ELEVEN

# ACTS 12:1-13:52

## To Asia Minor

The believers in Jerusalem have been forced by God's direct intervention to receive Gentiles into the Church on an equal basis with Jews (10:1-11:18). The believers in Antioch have been enthusiastically evangelizing Gentiles in their own city for some time (11:19-26). In 12:1-13:52, we see God at work among the Christians of both Jerusalem and Antioch, pushing the Church ever outward. As you read these chapters, try to imagine yourself in Peter's and Saul's shoes.

**For Further Study:** In your outline of Acts, write titles for 12:1-19, 12:20-24, 12:25-13:3, 13:4-12, and 13:13-52. Doing this before you study may help you see the details in light of the whole. You can always change or expand your outline after deeper study.

### Herod and the Church (12:1-24)

***King Herod*** (12:1). Herod Agrippa I, grandson of Herod the Great (Matthew 2:1-20) and nephew of Herod Antipas (Luke 23:6-12). Agrippa I was a boyhood friend of Gaius Caligula and Claudius. When Gaius became emperor in 37 AD, he awarded his friend a small tetrarchy in Palestine, and in 40 BC he deposed Antipas and gave his territory to Agrippa. When Gaius was assassinated in 41 BC, Agrippa was in Rome and helped to secure Claudius as emperor; Claudius rewarded him with the rest of Herod the Great's kingdom. Thus, Agrippa had friends in high Roman circles, and Judea had no Roman procurator or soldiers as long as Agrippa ruled.

Herod Agrippa was also popular with the Jews because he was a descendant of the right-

**For Thought and Discussion:** Why couldn't persecution prevent the gospel from spreading (12:1,24)?

**For Thought and Discussion:** Does chapter 12 suggest to you that John's brother James died because the believers did not pray for him (12:2)? If so, why? If not, why is this fact important?

**For Further Study:** Compare Acts 12:1-19,24 to 2 Timothy 2:9. How does the story of Peter illustrate the statement of Paul?

ful Jewish ruling house. He was more considerate of Jewish feelings than the Roman procurators like Pilate had been, and in Jerusalem he behaved like a devout Jewish king. In Caesarea, however, he was a typical oriental despot with a taste for Greek and Roman culture; his Gentile subjects detested him.[1] In 12:1-24 we see both sides of him: currying favor with the Jewish authorities in Jerusalem, and encouraging Gentiles to treat him as a god in Caesarea.

***Feast of Unleavened Bread*** (12:3). This seven-day festival in April immediately followed the one-evening feast of ***Passover*** (12:4). Therefore, the two were regarded as one festival, which was often called Passover.

Agrippa lived in the palace of Caesarea, but as a good Jew he was in Jerusalem for Passover. (Jesus' crucifixion had also been scheduled not to overlap Passover.)

***Mary*** (12:12). She was Mark's mother and Barnabas' aunt (Colossians 4:10).

***His angel*** (12:15). Apparently, some Jews believed that a person's guardian angel sometimes appeared in the person's likeness. Luke recorded the belief but did not say it was valid.

***James*** (12:17). James the brother of John was dead (12:2), so this was "James, the Lord's brother" (Galatians 1:19).[2] He was converted when Jesus appeared to him after the Resurrection (John 7:5, Acts 1:14, 1 Corinthians 15:7). James became a recognized leader of the Jerusalem church along with Peter (Acts 15:6-21, Galatians 2:9).

***Executed*** (12:19). This is what usually happened to guards who let their prisoners escape.

---

1. What part did the believers in Jerusalem have in Peter's escape from Herod (12:5)?

______________________________________

______________________________________

______________________________________

2. God saved Peter from being executed by Herod (12:6-11), but He allowed James to die (12:2). What conclusions about persecution, prayer, and deliverance can we draw from these facts?

________________________________________

________________________________________

________________________________________

________________________________________

________________________________________

________________________________________

________________________________________

________________________________________

**Optional Application:** Find out some specific names and groups of Christians who are suffering for the gospel, and pray for them (12:5).

**For Thought and Discussion:** What does chapter 12 show about God? About the Church?

**For Thought and Discussion:** Do you think Herod's death and its aftermath teaches a lesson? If so, what is it?

***Tyre and Sidon*** (12:20). The main cities of Phoenicia (modern Lebanon). Both were ports with mixed Gentile populations, and both depended on grain from Galilee for bread.[3]

***The appointed day*** (12:21). Herod Agrippa I died in 44 BC. The Jewish historian Josephus wrote that Herod held Roman games (athletics, etc.) in Caesarea in honor of Emperor Claudius. On the second day of the games, Herod arrived in a robe of silver threads that glittered in the sun. Herod gave a speech, and some Gentiles offered him the stock flattery for a ruler: "henceforth we agree that you are more than mortal in your being." After he accepted that flattery, Herod was seized with internal pain, was carried out, and died five days later.[4]

## Barnabas and Saul commissioned
(12:25-13:3)

***Finished their mission*** (12:25). See 11:27-30.

***The Holy Spirit said*** (13:2). Possibly through one or more of the prophets.[5]

**For Thought and Discussion:** What do you think should be the role of fasting in your life? In your church's life? Why? (*Optional:* See 1 Samuel 7:6, Ezra 10:6, Isaiah 58:1-14, Matthew 6:17-18, Acts 14:23.)

**For Thought and Discussion:** To what extent does 13:1-3 set an example we *must* follow, to what extent does it offer a good example we *may* follow, and to what extent is it a unique event? To what modern situations is it relevant? Support your opinion with Scripture.

**Optional Application:** How does 13:1-3 apply to a decision you are currently facing?

3. In your judgment, why were "worshiping the Lord and fasting" (13:2) both important preparations for hearing the Holy Spirit speak?

______________________________

______________________________

______________________________

______________________________

______________________________

4. Once the Spirit had spoken and the missionaries were prepared to leave, the believers fasted, prayed, and laid their hands on the two men (13:3). What was apparently the point of these actions?

______________________________

______________________________

______________________________

______________________________

## Cyprus (13:4-12)

***Seleucia*** (13:4). The seaport of Antioch. (See the map on page 20.)

***Cyprus*** (13:4). A large island in the Mediterranean, sixty miles from Seleucia. ***Salamis*** (13:5) was a Greek city on the island's east coast, with enough Jews to support several ***synagogues***.

***Paphos*** (13:6) was the capital of Cyprus, on the west coast.[6]

***Bar-Jesus*** (13:6). That is, "son of Joshua." Paul rejects this name and calls the sorcerer "son of the devil" (13:10, NASB).

***Proconsul*** (13:7). Cyprus was a senatorial province because of its important copper mines, so it was governed by a proconsul, an official of senatorial (ultra-elite) rank.[7]

***Saul . . . called Paul*** (13:9). As a Roman citizen, Saul had three Latin names: a first name, a family name, and a surname. Like the proconsul of Cyprus, his surname happened to be Paullus (spelled "Paulus" in Greek). As a Jew, he also had a Hebrew name, Saul (spelled "Saulus" in Greek). Luke calls him by his Hebrew name when he is among Jews (7:58-13:2) but shifts to his Latin name when he goes among Gentiles. This was probably how Paul used his names.[8]

Notice that until now Luke has written "Barnabas and Saul" because Barnabas has been the leader, but now he shifts to "Paul and Barnabas" to indicate that Paul takes the lead in evangelism. When the two return to Jerusalem, the order returns to "Barnabas and Paul" (15:12) because Barnabas is more recognized there. The order of names was a way of signifying seniority in ancient times.[9]

**For Thought and Discussion:** Summarize the Holy Spirit's role in 13:1-52, both explicit (13:2,4,9,52) and implicit. Record your thoughts on page 33.

**For Thought and Discussion:** Paul and Barnabas made a habit of preaching first in a synagogue whenever they arrived in a city (13:5,14, 44-46; 14:1; etc.). Why did they go to the Jews before the Gentiles (Acts 13:45-47; Romans 1:16, 2:9-10, 9:1-5, 10:1-3)?

## Pisidian Antioch (13:13-52)

**For Thought and Discussion:** Do you believe that a modern evangelist could convince people in the same way that Paul convinced the proconsul (13:6-12)? Could you? Why or why not?

***Perga*** (13:13). The capital of ***Pamphylia***, a district on the coast of Asia Minor.

***Pisidian Antioch*** (13:14). "The leading city in the area known as Phrygia Galatica,"[10] and "the hub of good roads and trade. The city had a large Jewish population. It was a Roman colony, which meant that a contingent of retired military men was settled there. They were given free land and were made citizens of the city of Rome, with all the accompanying privileges."[11] This policy of settling retired soldiers in colonies was designed to ensure pockets of loyal citizens in strategic spots throughout the Empire. The veterans were there partly to balance and control the volatile Greeks, Phrygians, Jews and others in this cosmopolitan city. Pisidian Antioch was 110 miles (five to eight days' walk) from Perga.

***Synagogue rulers*** (13:15). There was no ordained minister in a synagogue. Instead, one or more of the elders conducted services, kept order and cared for the synagogue building. These officers

**For Further Study:** Pay attention to the reaction of Roman officials to the gospel throughout Acts. Why was this important to Luke?

**For Further Study:** Compare Paul's speech in 13:16-41 to Stephen's in 7:2-53.

**For Thought and Discussion:** Why can a person be acquitted only by merciful forgiveness, never by justice according to the Law (13:38-39)? See Romans 1:18-3:20, 7:7-12.

were called rulers.

The synagogue service normally began with prayer, then followed with readings from the ***Law*** (the books of Moses, Genesis through Deuteronomy) and the ***Prophets*** (Joshua through Malachi). The readers then briefly interpreted and expounded the texts. The rulers chose the day's readers, and often invited educated visitors to have this honor.[12]

***As it is written . . . So it is stated . . .*** (13:33,35). Both Psalm 2 and Psalm 16 were originally written by or for David and the kings of his line. By Paul's time, most Jews already recognized that those psalms referred ultimately to the Messiah.[13]

***Justified*** (13:39). Legally acquitted of guilt. In Romans 3:21-22, Paul adds a further dimension of justification: the positive gift of righteousness, the restored relationship with God that flows from forgiveness and acquittal.[14]

---

5. In the first part of his sermon, Paul traces Israelite history. What episodes does he mention?

13:16-19 ______________________________

______________________________

13:20-22 ______________________________

______________________________

13:23-25 ______________________________

______________________________

13:26-31 ______________________________

______________________________

6. Next Paul explains the significance of these events. What has God promised the Jews that He has now fulfilled (13:32-37)?

______________________________

______________________________

7. What will happen if the Jews believe what Paul claims about Jesus (13:38-39)?

8. What happens when many of the Jews reject Paul's message (13:41-51)?

9. In Acts 13:47, Paul quotes Isaiah 49:6, which was originally addressed to the Servant of the Lord (see Acts 3:13, Isaiah 49:1-7). Why can Paul apply the Servant's commission to himself and Barnabas? (*Optional:* See, for example, John 20:21, Acts 9:15, 1 Corinthians 12:27.)

***God-fearing women of high standing*** (13:50). Judaism was especially attractive to Gentile women of the middle and upper classes. These women had enough wealth, education, and leisure to feel that traditional religion and social relations

**For Thought and Discussion:** Why did the Gentiles receive the gospel so much more eagerly than the Jews did? Why did the Jews find it so hard to accept that Jesus was the Messiah and that the Law could not justify a person? (Try to put yourself in the Jews' place, and consider what the Gospels tell us about the Jews.)

**Optional Application:** Does 13:47 express your mission? If so, what steps can you take to fulfill it better?

**Optional Application:** Do you act as though you can be justified in some other way than by sheer forgiveness (13:38-39)? Talk to God about this.

**For Thought and Discussion:** a. What does the confrontation between Paul and Elymas reveal about how the Holy Spirit convinced people to believe the gospel?

b. What does it reveal about how believers sometimes responded to opposition?

were unfulfilling. According to their various temperaments, dissatisfied women flocked either to Judaism or to the oriental cults. It was easier for a woman than a man to become a Jew, since women did not have to undergo circumcision.[15]

***Shook the dust from their feet*** (13:51). Jews shook the unholy dust from their feet when they left Gentile territory and entered Judea. Paul and Barnabas were saying that the unbelieving Jews of Antioch were Gentiles in God's sight, rejected from Israel because of their unbelief.[16] (See Luke 9:5.)

---

10. On pages 32-34, record what 12:1-13:52 reveals about the topics listed there.

11. Write down one or more insights from 12:1-13:52 that apply to your life.

_______________________________________

_______________________________________

_______________________________________

_______________________________________

_______________________________________

_______________________________________

_______________________________________

12. How can you begin to put one of these insights into practice with prayer and/or action this week?

_______________________________________

_______________________________________

_______________________________________

_______________________________________

_______________________________________

_______________________________________

13. List any questions you have about these chapters.

_______________________________________

_______________________________________

_______________________________________

_______________________________________

**Optional Application:** What would happen if you told someone about Jesus? Are you willing to suffer what James, Peter, and Paul did?

## For the group

**Warm-up.** Ask whether anyone in the group has tried discussing the gospel with an unbeliever since you began studying Acts. If anyone says yes, ask how that person responded and how the experience made the group member feel. If no one says yes, ask the group why they think this hasn't happened.

**Questions.** Focus on one or more of the following issues in chapters 12 and 13: why God answered the prayer to save Peter but didn't save James; how God punished Herod's sin; seeking guidance through prayer and fasting; the confrontation between Paul and the magician; how Jesus fulfilled Old Testament prophecy; why the evangelists took on the commission given to Jesus. Consider applying insights into prayer or fasting as a group.

**Pisidian Antioch.** Paul's sermon may be difficult for those who don't know the Old Testament well. If the group has trouble, explain that he is probably speaking on the day's readings from Scripture, but we don't know what the passages were. First he traces Israelite history briefly from the choice of Abraham through the sojourn in Egypt, the Exodus and desert wandering, and the conquest of the promised land under the judges (13:17-20). Then, Paul recalls, Israel asked for a king, and God gave Saul and then David (13:21-22). Paul's point is that Jesus (whom he proclaims in 13:23-31) is the fulfillment of God's promises regarding a king to inherit David's throne (13:32-37). After showing how Jesus fulfilled Psalm 2:7 and 16:10, Paul states the implications for his audience: forgiveness and acquittal are available through faith in Jesus (Acts 13:38-41).

**Worship.** Thank God for Jesus, the Son of God and Son of David, who fulfills all God's promises and makes forgiveness and justification available. Thank God also for answers to your prayers, just as He answered those who prayed for Peter.

## Travel in the Empire, part one

In 2 Corinthians 11:25-27, Paul barely alludes to the hardships of the road that Acts never mentions. An article by Jerome Murphy-O'Connor can help us appreciate just what Paul and other missionaries were willing to go through to bring the gospel to the ends of the earth.

Traveling from Thessalonica to Jerusalem today would take a few hours by plane, a few days by car or train. But none of these options existed for Paul. A wealthy man could have rented a carriage, but anything with wheels was beyond the means of a missionary-craftsman. Only military couriers road horses for more than local errands, for riding was a challenge in an era when "saddles were rudimentary, and stirrups unknown."[17] So, Paul was left with two alternatives: a ship by sea, or his two feet by land.

It could have been worse. Since about 30 BC when Augustus Caesar became emperor, Rome had been keeping reasonable order throughout its territories; no pillaging armies wandered the countryside, and highway robbers were curbed, if not eliminated. Also, in order to speed troop movements, the Romans had been building good stone roads on major arteries. About every twenty-two modern miles along a road there was at least an inn, if not a village or town, where travelers could sleep fairly safely.

Twenty-two miles a day was an average pace for a carriage, but a stiff one for a walker like Paul. If the road was hilly, the weather wet and muddy, or his morning start delayed, Paul would often have been unable to reach an inn by nightfall. At those times he would have been "in hunger and thirst, often without food, in cold and exposure" (2 Corinthians 11:27, NASB). Heat or illness could make him weak; snow could block a mountain pass; hail could hurt him; and

*(continued on page 123)*

*(continued from page 122)*

flooding could produce "danger from rivers" (2 Corinthians 11:26). The road from Tarsus to Galatia to Ephesus crosses the Anatolian plateau, which averages three thousand feet above sea level but is twice that in some sections; "extreme variations of temperature are the rule" there.[18] The mountains of northern Greece (Philippi to Thessalonica to Athens) would also have challenged Paul's stamina.

A common traveler could not expect free hospitality along the road, for country peasants were already fed up with Roman troops and officials. Such people could requisition any roadside dweller or his animals or carts to carry baggage (see Matthew 5:41). So, if Paul wanted food or a roof, he had to pay for it. Since a tentmaker was skilled in working all kinds of leather, Paul could earn a few coins mending another traveler's leather cloak, sandals, waterskin or wineskin, animal harness, or even camping tent. However, he could also find himself delayed by working all morning or all night. He could even "be commandeered by a soldier or official to repair the soldier's or official's equipment. For this, he was unlikely to be paid and all such work meant delay—another reason why Paul sometimes found himself far from where he planned to be at nightfall."[19]

Even an inn did not guarantee a peaceful snooze. "The average inn was no more than a courtyard surrounded by rooms. Baggage was piled in the open space, where animals were also tethered for the night. The drivers sat around noxious little fires fueled by dried dung, or slept on the ground wrapped in their cloaks."[20] If Paul had little money, he slept with them. If he had more, he rented a bed in a room along with several strangers who snored, or who might steal his leatherworking tools if he slept. He also shared his bed with the inevitable colony of bedbugs.

As a lone traveler, Paul was often "in danger from bandits" (2 Corinthians 11:26). Bears, wolves, boars, and other wild beasts provided more "dangers in the wilderness" (11:26, NASB). But there was also "danger in the city" (11:26)

*(continued on page 124)*

(continued from page 123)

for a stranger. In small towns where the provincial governor seldom visited, a few families tended to run the show. Paul was no aristocrat or wealthy merchant who could claim the governor's protection, so he was easily victimized by young hoodlums or unscrupulous townsmen. A companion or two like Barnabas and Timothy was invaluable both on lonely roads and in isolated towns.

(continued on page 158)

1. Marshall, page 207; Bruce, *New Testament History,* pages 258-264; Koester, *Introduction to the New Testament: Volume 1: History, Culture, and Literature of the Hellenistic Age,* page 397.
2. Those who believe that Mary bore only Jesus understand "brother" here to mean a near cousin; Jews did use the word in this way.
3. *The NIV Study Bible,* page 1669.
4. Josephus, *Antiquities,* translated by H. St. James Thackeray, in The Loeb Classical Library (Cambridge: Harvard University Press, 1928, 1956), book 19, chapters 343-350. See also Marshall, pages 211-213; Bruce, *New Testament History,* pages 262-264.
5. *The NIV Study Bible,* page 1669; Marshall, page 216.
6. Marshall, pages 217-218.
7. Marshall, page 217.
8. Bruce, *New Testament History,* pages 235-236; Marshall, page 220.
9. *The NIV Study Bible,* pages 1670, 1674.
10. Marshall, page 222.
11. *The NIV Study Bible,* page 1670.
12. Leon Morris, *The Gospel According to Saint Luke* (Grand Rapids, Michigan: William B. Eerdmans Publishing Company, 1974), page 106; *The NIV Study Bible,* pages 1503, 1555. See also Uuras Saanivaara, *Can the Bible Be Trusted* (Minneapolis, Minnesota: Osterhus Publishing House, 1983), pages 49-51.
13. *The NIV Study Bible,* pages 787-788, 799.
14. *The NIV Study Bible,* page 1671; Marshall, page 228.
15. Wayne Meeks, *The First Urban Christians* (New Haven: Yale University Press, 1983), pages 24-25.
16. Marshall, page 231.
17. Jerome Murphy-O'Connor, O. P., "On the Road and on the Sea with St. Paul," *Bible Review* (Washington, D. C.: Biblical Archaeology Society, Summer 1985), page 40.
18. Murphy-O'Connor, page 41.
19. Murphy-O'Connor, pages 41-42.
20. Murphy-O'Connor, page 42.

LESSON TWELVE

# ACTS 14:1-15:35

## Gentile Christians?

Paul and Barnabas are still on their mission, acting as "a light for the Gentiles" to "bring salvation to the ends of the earth" (13:47). Their view of the Church's mission will soon prove decisive for the whole of history. As you read 14:1-15:35, think about how those events have affected your life.

### Iconium, Lystra, Derbe (14:1-28)

***Iconium*** (14:1). "An important crossroads and agricultural center in the central plain of the province of Galatia."[1] It was ninety miles east of Pisidian Antioch on the Roman road.[2] Both Antioch and Iconium were in the district of Phrygia.

***Miraculous signs and wonders*** (14:3). The Holy Spirit was active through Paul and Barnabas, just as through Jesus and Peter (Luke 4:17-26; Acts 3:1-10, 14:8-10).

***Apostles*** (14:4,14). Luke has so far used this term for the Twelve who followed Jesus during his earthly life (1:21-22), but here Luke calls Paul and Barnabas apostles. As a friend of Paul, Luke was no doubt aware that Paul considered both himself and Barnabas to be apostles on the level of the Twelve (1 Corinthians 9:1-6; Galatians 1:1,12,15-17).[3] Also, Paul had received a direct

**For Thought and Discussion:** From the following verses, summarize the key features of Paul's missionary strategy on this trip: 13:14,46; 14:1-6,21-23. Why was each element important?

**For Thought and Discussion:** What are some of the assumptions about God or gods, miracles, creation, morality, the nature of man, etc. that your friends hold? Which of those beliefs are barriers to understanding and believing the gospel? How can you help them rethink those assumptions?

commission from Jesus (9:15-16) and both men had been performing the works of an apostle (14:3).

***Lycaonian cities*** (14:6). The missionaries escaped the lynch mob in Iconium by fleeing across the Phrygian border to the district of Lycaonia.[4] ***Lystra*** was "an insignificant village which had been made into a Roman colony in 6 BC, as part of a scheme for defense against local warlike tribes."[5] It was just eighteen miles from Iconium, so it was easy for the Jews to pursue the apostles (14:19). ***Derbe*** was sixty miles further on.

***Zeus . . . Hermes*** (14:12). An ancient local legend said that these two gods had once visited Phrygia disguised as mortals. Only one old couple on the Lycaonian border gave them hospitality. Later a flood drowned everyone in the region except that couple; they became guardians of a temple to Zeus and Hermes and changed into lofty trees when they died. The Lystrians were determined not to offend the gods again.[6]

---

1. The Lystrians reacted to the healing of the lame man like typical rural pagans of that time (14:8-13). What do you learn from this incident about the religious beliefs of those people—the assumptions that Paul and Barnabas had to overcome? (List as many observations as you can.)

______________________________

______________________________

______________________________

______________________________

______________________________

______________________________

2. Acts 14:15-17 gives us our first example of what Paul and Barnabas preached to purely Gentile audiences, as opposed to Jews, proselytes, and God-fearers. In addition to proclaiming Jesus,

what did the apostles have to explain to pagans that they didn't have to say to Jews and God-fearers?

______________________________________

______________________________________

______________________________________

______________________________________

______________________________________

______________________________________

3. What does 14:19-20 tell you about Paul's character?

______________________________________

______________________________________

______________________________________

______________________________________

---

***The kingdom of God*** (14:22). In a sense, the Kingdom is already among us (Luke 17:20-21). However, here Paul and Barnabas are referring to the future fulfillment of God's realm that believers will experience when they die or when Jesus returns.[7]

***Appointed*** (14:23). "Ordained" in KJV. This Greek word originally meant "to elect by a vote of raised hands."[8] It came to mean either to appoint or to elect, without regard to method. Thus, the word itself doesn't tell us whether Paul and Barnabas chose the elders, or whether the congregations elected them and the apostles approved them.[9]

---

4. When the apostles returned to Lystra, Iconium, and Antioch to strengthen and encourage the infant disciples, they warned them, "We must go through many hardships to enter the

**For Thought and Discussion:** What do your nonChristian friends need to understand about God before they can begin to understand the gospel? Is 14:15-17 the place to start, or do your friends need to begin with something else?

**Optional Application:** a. Put yourself in the place of the apostles in 13:50; 14:4-6,19-20. Would you have kept going? What enabled the apostles to do so?

b. Put yourself in the place of the new believers staying in those towns. Would you have withstood the pressure to abandon faith in Christ? What enabled the believers to stand firm?

kingdom of God" (14:22). From 13:50; 14:4-6,19-20 and from your own knowledge of bigotry, discrimination, and hostility, what hardships could the new Christians expect?

5. Despite all the hardships on their trip, what was Paul and Barnabas' verdict when they reported back to the church in Antioch (14:26-27)?

## Council at Jerusalem (15:1-35)

Paul had been a Pharisee, but when he recognized Jesus as the Christ, his attitude toward the Law began to change radically. However, there were Pharisees and other Jews who followed Jesus Christ but did not yet realize how His coming had affected the status of the Law. They continued to interpret God's Word in Scripture according to Jewish tradition. Also, it was ingrained in them from birth that the Law was the essence of moral good and holiness. Since God had commanded circumcision, the dietary laws, and the rest as "an everlasting covenant" (Genesis 17:13, Exodus 31:16), and since those laws were manifestations of holiness (Leviticus 20:25-26), these Jewish Christians could not imagine that God had set the laws aside. It followed that if the laws were God's desire for His people, then they were binding on Gentile as well as Jewish believers. What evidence was there that God had abandoned the laws?

Further, even if Gentile believers were exempt (these Jewish Christians reasoned), Jewish ones were not. Therefore, Jewish believers could not eat unclean food with Gentiles in fellowship meals. So, some argued, Gentile Christians should keep the laws in order to maintain fellowship with Jewish ones. Thus, there were two issues at stake: 1) Does God still require His covenant people to keep the Law of Moses (and the oral tradition)? and 2) Even if the Law is just a cultural preference for Jewish Christians, should Gentile Christians keep it anyway in order to keep peaceful fellowship?

In all this, the Jewish believers were partly concerned not to put barriers in the way of converting fellow Jews. The Antiochenes, of course, were concerned not to hinder Gentiles.[10]

6. How did the Church handle this major dispute between some Jewish believers and the Antiochene Christians (15:2,6,12,22-30)?

_______________________________________

_______________________________________

_______________________________________

_______________________________________

_______________________________________

7. Why did Peter support the Antiochene position? List his key reasons in 15:6-11.

_______________________________________

_______________________________________

_______________________________________

_______________________________________

_______________________________________

8. What evidence did Paul and Barnabas offer to defend their view that Gentiles could be saved without becoming Jews (15:4,12)?

_______________________________________

_______________________________________

**For Thought and Discussion:** Why do you think it was so important for the Church that Gentiles not be required to keep the Jewish Law (15:9-11,19)?

**For Thought and Discussion:** According to the council, what is necessary for salvation (15:9-11)? What isn't necessary?

**For Further Study:** If keeping the Law was not necessary for salvation, why did even Paul agree that the Gentiles should obey the rules of 15:20? (See Romans 14:1-4,13-23; 1 Corinthians 8:1-11:1.)

**For Thought and Discussion:** Is eating blood still wrong (such as in sausage, rare meat, or strangled poultry)? Why or why not? (See Romans 14:1-4,13-23.)

______________________________

______________________________

9. James was by now a leader of the Jerusalem congregation and known for his conservative Jewish practice (Galatians 2:11-12). What convinced James that Paul was right about the Gentiles and the Law (Acts 15:13-19)?

______________________________

______________________________

______________________________

______________________________

***Abstain*** (15:20). The council made four requirements regarding habits to which Gentiles were especially prone but which especially disgusted Jews. ***Sexual immorality*** was not only rampant in private affairs, but also a religious rite to honor certain gods. Most meat from non-Jewish butchers came from pagan temples, since only part of any sacrificed animal was burnt. Also, Gentile civic, social, and professional associations often held dinner parties in temples of patron gods. Thus, meat ***polluted by idols*** was hard to avoid. ***Strangled animals*** could not have the ***blood*** properly drained, as Jewish law required. All four requirements reflected the laws of holiness in Leviticus 17-18.[11]

10. What are the most important lessons the Jerusalem council's decision can teach us?

______________________________

______________________________

______________________________

______________________________

______________________________

______________________________

11. What one insight from 14:1-15:35 seems most relevant to you? How can you apply this insight through prayer and/or action?

______________________________________

______________________________________

______________________________________

______________________________________

______________________________________

______________________________________

12. Write any notes from 14:1-15:35 on the topics on pages 32-34.

13. List any questions you have about 14:1-15:35.

______________________________________

______________________________________

______________________________________

______________________________________

## For the group

**Warm-up.** Ask, "Think of one nonChristian you know. What does he or she believe about the origin of the world? If you don't know, how can you find out?" This question relates to 14:15-17.

**Iconium, Lystra, Derbe.** The geography of Acts can overwhelm modern readers with unfamiliar place-names. Part of the problem is that Luke mentions cities (Lystra), the districts that predated Roman rule (Phrygia), and the provinces that Rome created (Galatia). The provinces cut across the boundaries of the old districts, so the place names are confusing to non-experts. If necessary, get a good map of Paul's journeys in an atlas or study Bible. Even if you can't find a good map, explain that Pisidian Antioch, Iconium, Lystra, and Derbe were all in the province of Galatia—these were the churches who later received Paul's letter to the Galatians. (Galatia comprised several of the old districts, including

**Optional Application:** To what extent are your life-style and religious customs required for all Christians, and to what extent are they just cultural and personal preferences? Think of some specific examples. How should this distinction affect the way you view the practices of other Christians?

**For Thought and Discussion:** Missionaries still have to decide what aspects of people's lifestyles are inconsistent with Christianity and what aspects are acceptable even if they appear strange to Westerners. Can you think of any examples?

**Optional Application:** Meditate this week on the liberating truth decided at Jerusalem. Why is it important for you? How does it affect your actions?

**For Further Study:** Add 14:1-15:35 to your outline.

Lycaonia, part of Phrygia, and the *district* of Galatia.) Tell the group not to worry if the geography evades them; the point of the story should be clear anyway.

The actual issues of 14:1-28 are more important than the geography. For instance, the encounter with Gentiles in Lystra shows what can happen when we try to explain the gospel to people of another culture (even when those people live in our own country). What did you learn that you can apply to your evangelistic efforts?

**The council.** Make sure the group understands both sides of the issues the council addressed. (What were the issues? What was the conservative Jewish Christians' position, and why did they feel that way? What was the Antiochenes' view, and why?) Help everyone see the conservatives' point of view as well as Paul's. Consider how modern church debates resemble this one, and how the methods of Jerusalem can be applied today. Also, discuss why the principles decided at Jerusalem are important for you.

**Worship.** Praise God for creating and sustaining the world, for protecting infant churches, and for guiding difficult decisions that the Church faces. Thank Him for freeing you from the obligation to keep the Law and for accepting you purely because of faith, not performance.

1. *The NIV Study Bible,* page 1672.
2. Marshall, page 232.
3. Marshall, pages 233-234; *The NIV Study Bible,* page 1672; Dietrich Muller and Colin Brown, "Apostle," *The New International Dictionary of New Testament Theology,* volume 1, pages 379-386.
4. Luke was enough of a historian to have verified that Iconium was part of Phrygia rather than Lycaonia only between 37 and 72 AD; modern historians have until recently thought Luke was in error on this point. See Kent, page 116.
5. Marshall, page 236.
6. Kent, pages 116-117; Barclay, page 109.
7. Marshall, page 241.
8. Kent, page 118.
9. *The NIV Study Bible,* page 1673.
10. Marshall, pages 242-243.
11. *The NIV Study Bible,* page 1675. See also Marshall, pages 246-247,253.

LESSON THIRTEEN

# ACTS 15:36-17:15

## Paul and Silas

Since winter travel was hazardous, Paul and Barnabas spent a few months after the Jerusalem council teaching and preaching in Antioch. But others in the church could fill that role; Paul and Barnabas were called to spread the gospel elsewhere. When spring brought calm seas, it was time for another mission. Read 15:36-17:15 prayerfully, asking yourself how you would have responded to various circumstances if you had been in Paul's place.

**For Further Study:** On your outline, write titles for 15:36-41, 16:1-5, 16:6-10, 16:11-15, 16:16-40, 17:1-9, and 17:10-15.

**For Further Study:** Does disagreeing and parting company have to lead to anger and broken fellowship? Consider how Paul felt about Barnabas and Mark after parting from them (1 Corinthians 9:1-7, Colossians 4:10, Philemon 24, 2 Timothy 4:11). What do you learn about fellowship? Is there an example here for you?

### Strengthening the churches (15:36-16:5)

***Mark*** (15:37). We don't know why Mark left the team in Pamphylia (13:13), nor why Paul thought his desertion was so serious. We do know that Mark was blessed to have such a cousin as the Son of Encouragement, for after some years evangelizing with Barnabas, Mark proved himself a worthy saint. He worked with Peter in Rome and wrote his Gospel from Peter's memories (1 Peter 5:13); he helped Paul during the apostle's first imprisonment in Rome (Colossians 4:10, Philemon 24); he eventually impressed Paul so much that he asked Mark to come during his final days in prison (2 Timothy 4:11).

***Silas*** (15:40). He was the Silvanus mentioned as a partner in Paul's and Peter's letters (1 Thessa-

**For Thought and Discussion:** Why do you think the Antiochene missionaries felt it was important to go out in teams (Barnabas, Paul, and Mark; Barnabas and Mark; Paul and Silas; etc.)? What were the advantages for travel and evangelism? What does this team strategy tell you about fellowship/partnership in the gospel? How might this method apply to you?

**For Thought and Discussion:** Why did Paul return to churches he had already founded? What did he do there, and why were those things important (15:41, 16:4-5)?

lonians 1:1, 2 Thessalonians 1:1, 1 Peter 5:12). He was a prophet (Acts 15:32), a leader in the Jerusalem church trusted to relay the decision about the Gentiles (15:22,27), and a Roman citizen (16:37-38).

***Timothy*** (16:1). Since Paul called him a young man about fifteen years later (1 Timothy 4:12), Timothy must have been a teenager at this point. Since both Luke and Paul mentioned his mother's faith but not his father's (Acts 16:1, 2 Timothy 1:5), his father was probably not converted either to Judaism or Christianity, and he may well have been dead. Apparently on Paul's first visit to Lystra about two years earlier, Timothy's whole household had become Christians, including his mother and grandmother (2 Timothy 1:5).

Jews were not supposed to marry Gentiles, so Timothy was a child of a mixed marriage in everyone's eyes. He was legally Jewish and raised Jewish (2 Timothy 3:15), so he was probably somewhat excluded by his Gentile peers. However, perhaps because his father had forbidden a rite Greeks found disgusting, Timothy was not circumcised. Therefore, he was an outsider—illegitimate according to some schools—to Jews as well. Timothy would be a much more effective missionary if he were a full Jew rather than neither Jew nor Gentile, so Paul ***circumcised him*** (16:3).[1] Earlier, Paul had refused to circumcise another colleague, Titus, because Titus was a Gentile (Galatians 2:1-5). In that case, the rite would have meant that Titus had to become Jewish in order to be Christian.

***Decisions*** (16:4). The letter of Acts 15:22-29 was addressed only to the Christians in Syria and Cilicia, but Paul wanted to use it in the Galatian churches he had founded. Pisidian Antioch, Lystra, Iconium, and Derbe were all in the province of Galatia, and the believers there were probably the ones to whom Paul wrote his letter to the Galatians (either shortly before or shortly after the Jerusalem council). That letter had addressed the issue of whether Gentile Christians must keep the Law; now Paul had an official letter from Jerusalem confirming his position.

## Philippi (16:6-40)

***Phrygia and Galatia*** (16:6). The geography in Acts is hard for modern people to follow. One reason is that before Rome conquered Asia Minor (modern Turkey), the area was divided into ethnic districts: Phrygia, Galatia, Pisidia, Lycaonia, etc. However, when the Romans took over, they divided the region into provinces that ignored the old district boundaries. Thus, the province of Galatia included parts of Pisidia, Lycaonia, and Phrygia, as well as the district of Galatia. Another part of Phrygia was in the province of Asia, and so on. So, "Phrygia and Galatia" could well mean the Phrygian part of Galatia where Iconium and Antioch were.[2]

***Mysia*** (16:7) was a district in the northwest of the province of Asia, and ***Bithynia*** was a province just east of Mysia. See the map on page 20.

***Troas*** (16:8). "A Roman colony and an important seaport for connections between Macedonia and Greece on the one hand and Asia Minor on the other."[3] Paul later visited believers there several times (Acts 20:5-12, 2 Corinthians 2:12), but we don't know when or by whom the church was started.

***Macedonia*** (16:9). A Roman province north of Greece (see the map on page 20). Across it ran the Egnatian Way, the Roman road that connected the eastern half of the Empire (the Aegean Sea, Asia Minor, etc.) to the western half (the Adriatic Sea, Italy, etc.). With good winds, it took just two days to sail from Troas to the Macedonian seaport of ***Neapolis*** (16:11) at the beginning of the Egnatian, after an overnight stop on the island of ***Samothrace***.

***We*** (16:10-17). Evidently, Luke joined Paul's party in Troas and accompanied it to Philippi; the rest of chapter 16 is his eyewitness account. It is also possible that Luke incorporated part of someone else's travel diary into this section, but it is odd that he gave no warning of this and didn't bother to make the verbs consistent with

**For Thought and Discussion:** Why do you think trained leaders like Paul and Barnabas liked to take inexperienced youths like Mark and Timothy into their teams? Consider 2 Timothy 2:2. Is there a principle here that you or your church can apply?

**For Thought and Discussion:** In circumcising Timothy, Paul was accommodating Jewish culture in order to further the gospel (1 Corinthians 9:19-23). In refusing to circumcise Titus, Paul was refusing to accommodate Jewish culture because of a theological principle. Do you face any similar decisions to accommodate or not? If so, what should you do?

**For Thought and Discussion:** In what sense is the Holy Spirit "the Spirit of Jesus" (16:7)? What does this phrase tell you about the nature of God?

**Optional Application:** Does God ever guide you by closing doors (16:6) or by direct leading (16:9)? If so, name an example or two. If not, how does He guide you, if at all?

the rest of his carefully composed writing.[4] The "we" account ends when the mission team leaves Philippi (16:39-40) and begins again when Paul returns to Philippi five years later (20:5-28:16).

---

1. On page 33, write how the Holy Spirit guided Paul and his team in 16:6-10. (Also, observe what Luke calls the Spirit in 16:6,7,10.)

2. From your notes on page 33, what patterns do you see in the way the Spirit works in Acts 1:1-16:10? (What does He do? How does He make God's will known? What are His goals?)

______________________________

______________________________

______________________________

______________________________

______________________________

______________________________

______________________________

______________________________

______________________________

3. How are the Spirit's goals, activities, and methods in your life like and unlike those you have observed in Acts?

like ______________________________

______________________________

______________________________

______________________________

______________________________

______________________________

______________________________

unlike ______________________________

______________________________

______________________________

______________________________

______________________________

______________________________

______________________________

4. Describe at least one way in which you think your observations of Acts should affect the way you expect the Spirit to act in your life or the way you respond to Him when He does act or speak.

______________________________

______________________________

______________________________

______________________________

______________________________

5. How can you grow more responsive to God's guidance, in whatever forms He chooses to give it? Think of some specific steps you can take.

______________________________

______________________________

______________________________

______________________________

______________________________

______________________________

**For Thought and Discussion:** a. Some Christians feel they would be more obedient to God if they had direct guidance from Him, such as visions. In Acts, does God normally guide through visions? In what situations does He choose to use visions, and in what situations does He prefer other methods?

b. What can we conclude about the functions of direct and less direct revelation in the Christian life?

---

***Philippi*** (16:12). This city was ten miles down the Egnatian Way from Neapolis. It was the only one of the half-dozen Roman colonies mentioned in Acts that Luke specifically identified

**For Thought and Discussion:** a. Why was it necessary for God to open Lydia's heart to respond to Paul's message (16:14)?

b. What significance does this fact have for you personally, in your evangelism and in your prayers?

as such, perhaps because the reaction of Romans to the gospel was the big issue in Philippi (16:16-40). The Philippians were self-consciously Roman; their ***magistrates*** (16:20,22) had Roman titles and were accompanied by the traditional *lictors* who bore bundles of rods with which to administer judicial floggings.

Philippi was full of retired military men who tended to despise Jews,[5] so few Jews had settled there. Just ten adult circumcised males were required to form a synagogue, but Philippi had only a ***place of prayer*** (16:13) where women gathered. It was outside the city walls by the river Gangites, perhaps because synagogues were banned within the city limits, or possibly because the women needed water for ritual purification.[6]

***Thyatira*** (16:14). A city in the province of Asia, in the old district of Lydia (the woman may have been named after the district). Thyatira was famous for its production of crimson-purple dye and dyed cloth, made from the juice of the local madder root. Independent businesswomen were not uncommon, especially if their male relatives died and left them the family businesses. ***Lydia*** was no aristocrat, but she was wealthy enough to rent a house in Philippi where the missionaries could stay comfortably. She probably became ***a worshiper of God*** in Thyatira, where there was a sizable Jewish community.[7]

***Spirit by which she predicted the future*** (16:16). Literally, "a spirit, a Python." The pythonic spirit was a snake that supposedly inspired the prophetesses at Delphi to speak oracles.[8]

***Customs unlawful*** (16:21). "The Romans were officially not supposed to practice foreign cults, although in practice they might do this so long as these did not offend against Roman customs. The principle was clearly a flexible one which could be invoked as necessary." The real issue for the slave girl's owners was economic loss, but they appealed to the authorities' prejudice against Judaism, an "un-Roman" superstition.[9] (At this stage, the Romans did not yet see a distinction between Christianity and the other dozen or so Jewish sects.) Paul and Silas were in Philippi in about 50 AD, less than a year after Emperor Claudius expelled all Jews from Rome for causing disturbances (18:2); Roman scorn for Jews was at high tide.

***Stripped and beaten*** (16:22). This was common Roman practice. Legally, the magistrates should have imprisoned the missionaries until they could have their case heard before the proconsul of Macedonia, but the magistrates considered this a trivial case that required a swift, firm hand, not judicial niceties. They may have planned to expel the outsiders the next day (16:35-36,39). This, too, may not have been strictly legal, but two unpopular Jews, even Roman citizens, would have been fools to refuse to leave.[10]

***Inner cell . . . stocks*** (16:24). Men capable of exorcising spirits required maximum security. However, since the Romans did not have the Jewish law that limited the severity of beatings, Paul and Silas were probably scarcely able to move from blood loss and lacerated muscles. Sitting or lying with their feet fastened in stocks so that they could neither shift nor roll over must have been agony.

---

6. Bloody and battered in the stocks of a lightless prison, Paul and Silas spent the night "praying and singing hymns to God" (16:23-25). Why do you think they did this? (For instance, what attitudes toward self, God, circumstances, the other prisoners, or the jailer do these actions show?)

______________________________

______________________________

______________________________

______________________________

______________________________

______________________________

**Optional Application:** **How do you normally respond to persecution or pain? How can you adopt Paul and Silas's response and attitudes (16:23-25)? Look and pray for a specific chance to do this.**

**For Further Study:** Compare what Paul says in Romans 13:1-7 to what he practices in Acts. Does he practice what he preaches? How or how not? In what ways can you apply his teaching and example?

***About to kill himself*** (16:27). "If a prisoner escaped, the life of the guard was demanded in his place (see 12:19)."[11] Suicide was the accepted Roman alternative to the disgrace of execution, especially since the suicide's property went to his heirs but the executed man's went to the state. However, this jailer was too terrified by the supernatural power of his prisoners to think rationally; he didn't even check to see if they were gone or consider that the magistrates would hardly hold him responsible for an earthquake. He knew of the exorcism and the men's preaching, had heard Paul and Silas singing in the stocks, and was deranged at the divine power invoked by these holy men.[12]

***Without a trial*** (16:37). Roman citizens were exempt from beatings, and they had a much better chance than non-citizens of having the magistrates disciplined for denying them a trial.[13]

***Escort us*** (16:37). Paul and Silas had to establish their innocence in order to protect the believers in Philippi and to avoid a precedent of treating Christian missionaries with hasty harshness. The magistrates agreed to appease and exonerate the two Jews, but they still insisted that Paul and Silas leave Philippi (16:40), perhaps because they feared more anti-Jewish clamor from the local people.[14]

7. How did Paul and Silas deal with Roman officials in Philippi (16:35-39)?

______________________________

______________________________

______________________________

______________________________

8. Why do you think they didn't just leave submissively? What principles for dealing with authority do their actions suggest? (You might make a note of this on page 33.)

______________________________

## Thessalonica (17:1-9)

***Amphipolis*** (17:1). A city one day's travel on horseback (33 miles) west of Philippi on the Egnatian Way. ***Apollonia*** was 27 miles further, and ***Thessalonica*** was another 35 miles west. Paul and Silas passed over the former two cities (by the Spirit's guidance or human planning?) to concentrate their evangelistic efforts on Thessalonica.

Thessalonica was a port city, the seat of Roman government in the province of Macedonia, and therefore the largest city in the province. It was a free city, governed by an assembly of citizens in the Greek tradition, rather than by aristocrats in the Roman style (the ***crowd*** of 17:5 is the *demos* in Greek, from which we get the word *democracy*, "rule by the people"). Non-Roman *politarchs* (the ***city officials*** of 17:6) were the magistrates. However, both the politarchs and the popular assembly probably took an oath to obey the emperor that empowered and required them to judge charges of treason (17:7-9).[15]

***Jealous*** (17:5). ("Envy" in KJV.) The Jews were trying to attract prominent Gentiles to the synagogue, but in Paul's preaching these Gentiles found the attractive spiritual aspects of Judaism without the burdensome laws like circumcision. Even some Jews were drawn to what orthodox Jews regarded as heresy and blasphemy.

***Caused trouble all over the world*** (17:6). The KJV translation "turned the world upside down" could be taken as unintentional praise, but the accusers were in fact charging the Christians

**For Further Study:** a. Why did the Christ have to die and rise (Acts 17:3)? See Leviticus 16:15-17, 20-23; Isaiah 53:1-12; Romans 6:1-14; Hebrews 9:11-10:18.

b. Why did the Jews find the idea of a killed and raised Christ so repugnant?

**For Thought and Discussion:** Compare the way the apostles dealt with persecution in 13:46-51, 16:37, and 17:10. How were the circumstances different? Why do you think each response was appropriate to each circumstance?

with subversion and sedition (17:7). At that time (about 50 AD), the Romans were having trouble with Jews all over the Empire. In Judea, Jewish terrorists were assassinating Jews who collaborated with Rome, and there were numerous messianic groups in other provinces. Uproar in the Jewish community had already led Emperor Claudius to expel all Jews from Rome in 49 BC (18:2). Back in 41 BC, Claudius had to quell riots between Greeks and Jews in Alexandria. Neither the Romans nor the Thessalonians were equipped to distinguish Paul's messianic preaching from other Jewish doctrines, so they lumped the Christians together with other Jewish troublemakers. Paul's presence had indeed caused a riot both in Philippi and now in Thessalonica. Besides, Paul was preaching that a man executed by Rome for proclaiming Himself king of the Jews was in fact Lord of the world (16:31, 17:7). Paul was also predicting that this Jesus would return and replace the Roman government (1 Thessalonians 1:10); predictions of this kind were politically dangerous and were punishable by death according to imperial ***decrees*** (17:7).[16]

***Post bond*** (17:9). "Taken security" in RSV. Jason had to pay a fee and guarantee that the missionaries would leave and not return; otherwise, Jason "would face the confiscation of his properties and perhaps even death"[17] for disturbing the peace.

---

9. In response to the gospel, Lydia and Jason both invited the missionaries to stay in their homes (16:15, 17:7). They welcomed at least four virtual strangers for indefinite periods of weeks or months. What kinds of trouble and expense were they risking by doing this (consider 16:20-22, 17:5-9)?

______________________________

______________________________

______________________________

______________________________

10. What can Lydia and Jason teach us about Christian fellowship/partnership?

## Berea (17:10-15)

*Berea* (17:10). Instead of continuing westward on the Egnatian Way, Paul and Silas detoured south 50 miles to Berea. The Way would have been the logical route to take if Paul had been going to Rome, but that was impossible because Claudius had expelled all Jews. Paul may have been hoping to return to Thessalonica, but "Satan stopped us" he wrote later (1 Thessalonians 2:17-18). It soon became clear that Macedonia was too hot for Paul just now, so he sailed to Athens (Acts 17:13-15).

11. How did the Berean Jews respond differently to Paul's message than the Thessalonian Jews did (17:5,11)?

**For Further Study:** Write on page 33 what you observe from 16:35-39 and 17:6-10 about dealing with authorities.

**For Further Study:** In Luke 8:4-15, Jesus told a parable about four kinds of soil, comparing people who respond to the gospel in different ways to different kinds of soil. How do the Thessalonians and Bereans illustrate this parable?

**For Further Study:**
a. Study Paul's letters to the Thessalonians (written about a year later) in light of Acts 17:1-15.

b. Study his letter to the Philippians (written about ten years later) in light of Acts 16:11-40.

**Optional Application:** How can you imitate the Bereans' response to new teaching?

12. Why was the Bereans' reaction the best way to deal with new and startling teaching?

13. Look back at questions 1 through 12 and the "Optional Application" questions in this lesson. What one insight from 15:36-17:15 would you like to apply to your own circumstances?

14. With what prayers and actions will you begin to put this insight into practice this week?

15. List any questions you have about 15:36-17:15.

## For the group

**Warm-up.** To help the group identify with Paul and Silas in the Philippian jail, ask, "Have you ever had to spend the night in pain? How did you spend the time?"

**Read and summarize.**

**Strengthening the churches.** Some people feel strongly that either Paul or Barnabas was wrong in 15:36-39. We've made this question optional because most of the necessary facts aren't given, but you can certainly discuss the matter if you like. A more serious question is whether Paul was right to circumcise Timothy. Help the group understand why he did it, then evaluate his decision and look for similar decisions in your lives.

**Philippi, Thessalonica, Berea.** The issues here are how God guides people, the grace He gives to enable a person's faith, attitudes under persecution, the believers' response to official opposition, fellowship, and how the Bereans responded to new teaching. Choose one or two of these to focus on in your discussion.

**Wrap-up.** The last few lessons have contained a great deal of scene-setting background. Reassure the group that it is not necessary to learn it all, since the background is meant only to help Acts come alive for you.

**Worship.** Thank God for guiding and sustaining His evangelists despite opposition from many sides. Thank Him for people like Paul, Silas, Timothy, Lydia, and Jason. Praise Him in the midst of your sufferings, as Paul and Silas did.

**For Further Study:** What charges were made against the evangelists in Philippi and Thessalonica (16:20-21, 17:7)? What were the real reasons each group objected to the missionaries? How are those reasons like and unlike modern people's reasons for protesting against and suppressing Christianity?

1. Marshall, pages 259-260; *The NIV Study Bible,* page 1676; Bruce, *Paul,* pages 213-216.
2. Marshall, pages 261-262; Bruce, *Paul,* page 217.
3. *The NIV Study Bible,* page 1676.
4. Marshall, pages 44, 263-264; Bruce, *Paul,* page 218.
5. Ralph P. Martin, *Philippians* (Grand Rapids, Michigan: William B. Eerdmans Publishing Company, 1976), pages 5-6.
6. Marshall, pages 266-267.
7. Bruce, *Paul,* page 220; Marshall, page 267.
8. Marshall, page 268; Bruce, *Paul,* pages 220-221.
9. Marshall, page 270.

10. Marshall, pages 271, 274-275; Bruce, *Paul,* page 221.
11. *The NIV Study Bible*, page 1678.
12. Marshall, page 272.
13. Marshall, pages 274-275.
14. Marshall, page 274-275.
15. Bruce, *Paul,* pages 223-226; Marshall, pages 276-278.
16. Bruce, *Paul,* pages 225-226. Jewish attacks on Christianity may have been behind the trouble in Rome and Alexandria; the historian Suetonius recorded around seventy years later that the trouble in Rome was started "at the instigation of Chrestus," a possibly garbled account of what happened. See Bruce, *New Testament History,* page 297.
17. *The NIV Study Bible,* page 1679. See also Marshall, page 280.

LESSON FOURTEEN

# ACTS 17:16-18:23

## Athens and Corinth

Paul left Macedonia in a hurry when it became clear that the Jewish vigilantes there were not going to leave him alone. Silas and Timothy were able to go discreetly back to Philippi, leaving Paul to wait alone in Athens. But Paul was not one to sit idly, paralyzed by memories of persecution and prospects of ridicule, even in a sophisticated city like this one. So, despite or even because of the conflict in Macedonia, the gospel came to Greece, the cradle of the culture that dominated the known world.

As you read about Paul's time in Athens and Corinth in 17:16-18:23, try to put yourself into those cities in Paul's place, or think of yourself as one of the people who heard Paul. Ask God to show you Himself at work.

### **Athens** (17:16-34)

***Athens*** (17:16). The golden age of Athenian art, literature, philosophy, and democracy was five centuries earlier, and by Paul's time the city's pride rested on faded laurels. It had a major university and was the first home of the four chief philosophical schools, but the best students went to Alexandria and other centers. However, Athens was still a beautiful city and a free ally of Rome with at least the forms of democratic government, and the name of Athens retained a certain mystique.[1]

**For Further Study:** Contrast Epicurean and Stoic beliefs (about God, the origin of things, man, afterlife, and how people should live) with what Paul says in 17:24-31.

**For Thought and Discussion:** Do you know any people who hold views like those of the Epicureans or Stoics? What is attractive about those beliefs, and how can a Christian counter them?

***Epicurean*** (17:18). These were followers of Epicurus (341-270 BC), who taught that:

a. Everything that exists is made of particles of matter called "atoms."

b. Therefore, there is no immortal soul; when you die, your atoms disintegrate and form other objects.

c. Therefore, you don't need to fear death or punishment after death.

d. The gods, too, are made of matter; they live "in the spaces between the worlds, enjoying perfect blessedness, undisturbed by concern for mankind or worldly affairs."

e. Therefore, you don't need to fear or pray to the gods.

f. The highest good for a person is "pleasure"—not sensuality, but "peace of mind, freedom from disturbing cares." The pleasures of the flesh should be minimized because they often lead to pain; instead, one should "live unobtrusively" and not stick one's neck out.[2]

***Stoic*** (17:18). This group was founded by Zeno (335-263 BC), who taught in a *stoa* or covered porch in Athens. Stoics believed that:

a. Man is completely a part of and a microcosm of nature. Just as creative Reason (*logos*) imposes order on matter, so it should govern a person's life. The best way to live is in harmony with nature. Fate is unavoidable, determined, but not capricious; thus, a person should seek to cooperate with and submit to destiny.

b. Self-sufficiency is the highest human virtue; one should tolerate and endure life as far as possible, then commit suicide with dignity if things become unbearable.

c. God is not a person, but rather the soul of the universe and a spark in each thing.

d. The soul survives when the body dies, but it becomes part of the world-soul instead of keeping an individual personality.[3]

***Babbler*** (17:18). Literally, "seed-picker"—a bird that goes about picking up scraps in gutters. This was Athenian slang for a person who hangs around lectures picking up scraps of learning and parrots them without understanding.[4]

It was fashionable among cultured persons all over the Empire to write and speak in the style of the classical Athenians of four to eight centuries earlier. The common Greek spoken by men like Paul was derived from this classical "Attic" Greek, but any aristocrat could tell in a second who was and wasn't one of them by the sort of Greek he spoke and wrote.[5] Paul didn't use the complex grammar, pure accent, and sophisticated jargon of the genteel philosophers, so he was obviously a boor from some backwater province. (Paul's Jewish legal and theological training and his sharp mind were irrelevant to the Greek philosophers.)

**For Thought and Discussion:** How should we deal with intellectuals who consider Christians "babblers"? Should we adopt the language of current philosophy? Should we ignore intellectuals?

***Areopagus*** (17:19). Literally, "Hill of Ares," the god of war (Mars to the Romans). Before Athens became democratic, the governing council of the city used to meet on that hill south of the marketplace. Its authority was reduced under the democracy, but "it retained considerable prestige and continued to exercise responsibility in the realm of religion, morals and homicide."[6] In Paul's time, the Council of the Areopagus met in the Royal Portico in one corner of the marketplace.

***Religious*** (17:22). This Greek word could mean "pious" in a good sense or "superstitious" in a bad sense. Paul's audience would have to listen to find out whether he was being complimentary, critical, or ironic.[7]

***Some of your own poets*** (17:28). "In him we live and move and have our being" is from the Cretan poet Epimenides. "We are his offspring" is found in works both by Aratus and Cleanthes. All these poets were popular with Stoics, who understood the God in their poems to be the Logos—divine Reason, the world-soul.[8]

---

1. How does Luke describe Athens and its people (17:16,21)?

_______________

_______________

**For Thought and Discussion:** Why do you suppose it is often so hard for sophisticated people to accept the gospel? How can Christians help them?

**Optional Application:** How would you have felt, faced with an audience like the Athenians? Would you rather be persecuted, ridiculed, or dismissed with polite amusement? How can you adopt Paul's attitude toward the ways people reacted to him?

______________________________________

______________________________________

______________________________________

2. What did the cultured men think of Paul, and why (17:18,32)?

______________________________________

______________________________________

______________________________________

______________________________________

______________________________________

3. Put yourself in Paul's place, addressing well-born, well-dressed intellectuals in an age where class distinctions were stone walls between people. Why was Paul able to face those men confidently? (*Optional:* See 1 Corinthians 1:18-31.)

______________________________________

______________________________________

______________________________________

______________________________________

______________________________________

4. When invited to speak to the prestigious Areopagus (17:24-31), what did Paul say about . . .

the nature, character, and attributes of God?

______________________________________

______________________________________

______________________________________

______________________________________

______________________________________

______________________________________

the nature of man? ______________________

idols? ______________________

Jesus? ______________________

5. How was this speech in Athens different from what Paul said to Jews (9:20,22; 13:16-41; 17:2-3)?

**For Thought and Discussion:** What do you think was Paul's purpose in his opening words (17:22-23)? Why did he quote Greek poets that philosophers liked (17:28)? Why did he discuss the nature of God, rather than the identity of Jesus?

**For Thought and Discussion:** Why is resurrection central to the gospel? (*Optional:* See Romans 1:2-4, 6:8-11; 1 Corinthians 15:12-58.)

**Optional Application:** How do nonChristians you know feel about the idea of resurrection, as opposed to reincarnation, the immortality of the soul, or permanent death? How can you help others overcome feelings of scorn or indifference?

**For Thought and Discussion:** How was Paul's speech in Athens like and unlike the one in Lystra (14:14-17)? Can you think of reasons for the similarities and differences?

6. Why do you think Paul addressed the Athenians differently than Jews? (What principle of evangelism was he practicing, and why is it important?)

7. Is anything in 17:16-34 relevant to your life? If so, what is relevant and why?

## Corinth (18:1-17)

***Corinth*** (18:1). See the map on page 20. A Roman army leveled ancient Corinth in 146 BC after a revolt, but Julius Caesar rebuilt it a century later as a colony for Roman veterans. Corinth quickly regained its former prosperity and character.

Situated on the Isthmus of Corinth, the city commanded both the land route through Greece and the sea trade from the Aegean Sea to the Adriatic Sea. From Cenchrea (18:18), the port east of Corinth, ships or cargoes were dragged three-and-a-half miles on a sort of wooden railroad track to Lechaeum, the port west of Corinth. In that way, sailors could avoid the time-consuming and hazardous trip around the Peloponese (the Greek peninsula). This system made Corinth a hub for traders, tourists, and business travelers.[9]

The temple of Aphrodite was one of Corinth's chief attractions for sailors and tourists passing through. It housed "a Hellenized form of the Syrian cult of Astarte,"[10] a fertility goddess. At the temple were at least a thousand male and female slaves dedicated to holy prostitution for men of whatever taste. This institution and the general tenor of the town prompted the Greek verb "to Corinthianize," which meant "to practice sexual immorality."

Corinth's population of some 250,000 free persons plus 400,000 slaves included not only Roman colonists, but also Greeks, Jews, Syrians, and other nationalities crowded together into just a few bustling square miles.[11]

***Aquila . . . Priscilla*** (18:2). Because Luke does not mention them converting and because Paul made a business partnership with them, they were probably already Christians when they met Paul. Christianity had undoubtedly reached Rome by this time, since it was the Empire's number one crossroads.[12]

***Tentmaker*** (18:3). Tents were made of goat's hair cloth or of leather, so this term could also mean "leather-worker" in general. Paul followed the Jewish custom that a rabbi did not charge for religious duties, but supported himself with a trade.[13]

***Silas and Timothy came*** (18:5). They brought money from the Philippian church, so that Paul could devote himself to preaching without burdening the Corinthians (2 Corinthians 11:9; Philippians 1:3-5, 4:15).

***Gallio*** (18:12). The son of the famous rhetor M. A. Seneca, and the brother of the Stoic philoso-

**Optional Application:** How can you shape your presentation of the gospel to suit the particular people you deal with?

**Optional Application:** What difference do Jesus and the Resurrection, Paul's teaching about God, or some other aspect of his sermon make to your life? In what specific ways should you respond to what Paul says?

**For Thought and Discussion:** How did the Philippians show their partnership/fellowship with Paul (18:5)? Is this an example for you to follow?

**Optional Application:** Pray for Christians in countries where the legal status of the Church is shaky. Ask God to move the authorities to tolerate Christianity more. (Choose one country, and pray regularly for its Christians and officials this week.)

pher L. A. Seneca. He was considered good-tempered and just, but ill health made his tenure over Greece brief.

The Jews accused Paul of urging religious practices that broke Roman law, but Gallio decided Paul's doctrine was just a variety of Judaism, a legal religion. This decision by an important Roman magistrate set a precedent for several decades: Christianity was a Jewish sect, so it was as legal as Judaism. That is, highborn Romans were discouraged from fully converting to Judaism, but the state seldom cared if low-born folk or provincials joined foreign religions. Religious clubs were mistrusted and Jews were considered peculiar, but Judaism was tolerated as an ancient and venerable religion. If Gallio had decided against Paul, Christianity might have been outlawed all over the Empire.[14]

***Turned on Sosthenes*** (18:17). The Greek grammar allows three possibilities: 1) The Greeks vented their anti-Jewish feelings on him, since Gallio had declined to intervene; 2) the Jews beat their leader because he had failed to present their case well enough; or 3) the Jews beat him because he had converted to Christianity and Gallio would not interfere in Jewish squabbles.[15]

---

8. What did God promise Paul in Corinth (18:9-10)?

______________________________

______________________________

______________________________

______________________________

9. How did Paul respond to that promise (18:11)?

______________________________

______________________________

______________________________

______________________________

10. How did God keep His promise (18:12-17)?

11. What do the events of 18:1-17 tell you about God?

12. Describe at least one way in which 18:1-17 is relevant to your life. Is there a promise, an example, or an insight about God that you might take to heart?

13. Consider questions 7 and 12, and the "Optional Applications" in this lesson. What one aspect of 17:16-18:17 would you like to focus on for application this week?

**For Thought and Discussion:** Does God still use secular officials to further the gospel, as He did in 18:2,14-16? If so, how?

**Optional Application:** Has God ever made any promises to you similar to the one in 18:9-10? If so, has He been faithful? How should you act in light of that promise?

**For Further Study:** Write into your outline what 17:16-34 and 18:1-17 contribute to the story of Acts.

14. What prayer and/or action will be part of your attempt to grow in this area by God's grace?

15. On pages 32-34, record what you learned about those topics from Paul's time in Athens and Corinth.

## Corinth to Ephesus to Antioch (18:18-23)

***Vow*** (18:18). "Jews made vows to God either in thankfulness for past blessings (such as Paul's safekeeping in Corinth) or as part of a petition for future blessings (such as safekeeping on Paul's impending journey); the present context inclines toward the former interpretation. A temporary Nazirite vow involved abstinence from alcohol and also from cutting one's hair. Its conclusion was marked by shaving one's hair completely off and offering a sacrifice in the temple at Jerusalem" (Numbers 6:1-21, Acts 21:17-26).[16]

Thus, a Jewish vow was not a promise to God to do something in one's own strength; Paul knew the truth of John 15:5, 2 Corinthians 12:9-10, and Philippians 4:13. Rather, the vow was the way a person expressed great thankfulness according to the Jewish custom in which Paul had been raised.

***Went up*** (18:22). Since Jerusalem was in the mountains, people spoke of "going up to" Jerusalem and "going down from" Jerusalem. Verse 22 probably means that Paul went to Jerusalem to offer the sacrifice that ended his vow and to visit the church.[17]

---

16. List any questions you have about 17:16-18:23.

____________________

____________________

____________________

____________________

## For the group

**Warm-up.** In his Athenian speech we find how Paul dealt with intellectuals. To help the group identify with Paul, ask, "How comfortable are you with people you consider intellectuals? Why do you feel this way?"

**Athens.** Have several people describe what Athens and the Athenians were like. Ask for some modern comparisons. Help the group feel the situation Paul was in. Then discuss what he said and why it was suitable for the Athenians, and possibly for modern audiences.

Use question 4 to be sure that everyone understands the points of doctrine Paul was teaching.

**Corinth.** Gallio's decision may not seem relevant to the group, but help everyone see why it was important to the early Christians. The Romans were suspicious of new religions, but they tolerated old ones like Judaism. Church-state relations are different now, but they are still a major issue. Does God still use unwitting secular authorities to protect the Church?

**The vow.** Some people feel strongly that Paul was wrong to make a vow in the Jewish manner (18:18) because he was released from the Law. Others think there was nothing wrong with expressing gratitude in the traditional way. We haven't addressed this issue becuse it involves people's interpretations of all that the New Testament says about the Law. Look at some commentaries and the whole tenor of the New Testament if you decide to deal with this question.

**Worship.** Pray for intellectuals and for evangelists in countries where the legal status of Christianity is shaky and dangerous. Thank God for protecting Christians in your country and others. Praise Him for what Paul says about Him in 17:24-31.

## Travel in the Empire, part two

With land travel so slow and hazardous, one might think people would have traveled by sea whenever possible. However, sea voyaging carried its own hardships.

When sailing southeast from Rome to Alexandria, ships covered several thousand miles in ten to twenty days.[18] That was because the prevailing winds in the sailing season came mostly from the northwest, sometimes from the west or northeast. But ships had shallow keels, no rudders, and only one sail, so they could not sail into or near the wind. Therefore, sailing west from Alexandria or Caesarea to Rome, Corinth or Ephesus was exasperating. Paul usually walked west across Asia Minor and sailed back east.

Passenger ships were rare; cargo ships took passengers when they had room. Paul would have had to find one going in his direction, haggle with the owner over the fee, then wait until the captain judged both the winds and the omens to be favorable. (The sea was so fickle that sailors were even more superstitious than landsmen, and even they were obsessed with astrology and omens by our standards.) On board, passengers supplied their own food—the captain would generously furnish water. Passengers took turns cooking their food in the galley after the crew was fed. "The fire might be doused by a stray wave, or rough conditions might mean the fire had to be extinguished before passengers had finished cooking, since loose live coals could do irreparable damage to a wooden boat in a very

*(continued on page 159)*

(continued from page 158)

short time."[19] There was no way to refrigerate foods like meat, so ships usually planned to dock and resupply every few nights (every night if possible). However, if a storm or long voyage delayed docking, only grain would be edible.

Few ships had cabins, so passengers lived on deck with only the sail for shade and shelter. Experienced travelers brought tents, for the vessel might dock at a port with no inn or at a small uninhabited cove. Wise travelers also went in pairs or groups to guard from theft or abuse.

Paul wrote, "Three times I was shipwrecked, I spent a night and a day in the open sea" (2 Corinthians 11:25). Shipwreck and partial ship damage were common. Many people considered it utter madness to travel by sea, for if one didn't encounter a storm, then one might run into something in the water or just snap a plank in the hull. Ancient vessels were so clumsy that they often couldn't maneuver to pick up survivors of a wreck, and there was no way to send an SOS anyway.

Violent storms made sailing in winter suicidal. Storms could also flair up suddenly in March, April, September, and October, but ships often took the risk in those months.

At best, sea travel was faster than walking. For many people, however, a voyage was a nightmare of seasickness if not a battle for their lives. Somehow, the risks seemed worthwhile to Paul; in addition to trudging about 1,795 miles overland on his missionary journeys, he also logged about 1,290 miles by sea besides his voyage as a prisoner to Rome.[20]

1. Bruce, *Paul,* pages 237-238; Marshall, page 283.
2. Bruce, *New Testament History,* pages 41-42.
3. Bruce, *New Testament History,* pages 44-47.
4. Marshall, page 284; *The NIV Study Bible,* page 1680.
5. John T. Townsend, "Ancient Education," *The Catacombs and the Colosseum,* pages 148-149, 152.
6. Bruce, *Paul,* page 238.
7. Marshall, page 285; *The NIV Study Bible,* page 1680.
8. Marshall, page 289.
9. *The NIV Study Bible,* page 1732; Bruce, *Paul,* page 250.
10. Bruce, *New Testament History,* page 314.
11. *The NIV Study Bible,* pages 1732-1733.

12. *The NIV Study Bible*, page 1681.
13. Marshall, page 293.
14. Bruce, *New Testament History,* pages 316-317; Marshall, pages 297-298.
15. Marshall, pages 298-299; *The NIV Study Bible,* page 1681.
16. Marshall, page 300; *The NIV Study Bible,* page 1682.
17. Marshall, page 301; *The NIV Study Bible*, page 1683.
18. Murphy-O'Connor, page 46.
19. Murphy-O'Connor, page 46.
20. Murphy-O'Connor, page 41 gives a breakdown of these distances.

LESSON FIFTEEN

# ACTS 18:24-19:41

## Ephesus

When Paul passed through Ephesus on his way to Jerusalem and Antioch, he left Priscilla and Aquila there to begin building a church. Ephesus was the queen of the rich Roman province of Asia. Through her port passed goods from China and the eastern provinces bound for Italy. Wide avenues, huge public buildings and squares, and luxurious private homes were designed to impress tourists.

A hundred local aristocrats owned most of the land around Ephesus and controlled the city government. However, the strength of the city was its large class of merchants, businessmen, and craftsmen. These people might be barely better fed than day laborers, nearly as wealthy as aristocrats, or somewhere in between, but none of them had any say in the government unless he was a "client" of one of the ruling hundred.

This working/business class was probably the group among whom Priscilla and Aquila began to explain their faith. God did not leave the couple to be the only missionaries in the city; they had first Apollos and later Paul as partners. As you read 18:24-19:41, ask the Holy Spirit to show you what He wants you to see.

## Apollos and the twelve disciples

(18:24-19:7)

Here Luke records two separate incidents side by side, probably for comparison.

**For Thought and Discussion:** How did Priscilla, Aquila, and Apollos show their fellowship/partnership with Paul in 18:18-28? List all the ways you observe. (See also Paul's words in 1 Corinthians 3:5-9.)

**Optional Application:** Why are baptism into Jesus and the indwelling of the Holy Spirit important in your life? How do your attitudes and actions reflect those events? How could your life better reflect those things?

---

***Alexandria*** (18:24). The Museum of Alexandria attracted the premier scholars of the Empire, and allegorical interpretation of the ancient pagan myths was the up-to-date form of literary criticism. Therefore, it was fashionable among Alexandria's large and sophisticated Jewish population to see the Scriptures as allegory; learned men found hidden inner meanings in the Law and the Prophets that only the wise could discern. We know nothing about the beginnings of Christianity in Alexandria, but it is not surprising that the gospel may have gotten a bit confused in that philosophical environment.[1]

***The baptism of John*** (18:25). Luke 3:1-18 portrays John's ministry. His was ***a baptism of repentance*** (Acts 19:4), signifying a recognition of one's sin and a desire to change and be forgiven, but John only pointed toward the fuller baptism into Jesus.

***Achaia*** (18:27). The province of which Corinth was the capital.

***Disciples*** (19:1). That is, Paul thought they were followers of Jesus (and perhaps they thought they were, too), but Paul soon found they believed in some form of the teaching of John the Baptist. They had faith that the Messiah was coming, but they didn't know the full story about Jesus and the Spirit.[2]

---

1. Both Apollos and the disciples Paul met had a similar gap in their information about the gospel. What did they not know (18:25, 19:2-3)?

_______________________________________

_______________________________________

_______________________________________

2. Why was it essential to be baptized in the name of Jesus, not just for repentance as John had done? (See Romans 6:3-11.)

_______________________________________

**With great fervor** (18:25). Literally, "with fervor in the spirit" or "in the Spirit." Apollos was not rebaptized, while the others were (18:26, 19:5); the reason may have been that Apollos had fairly accurate faith and had received the Holy Spirit, while the others had not (18:25, 19:2).

3. Why was it necessary to receive the Holy Spirit? (See John 3:5-6, 14:26; Romans 8:1-17,26-27.)

4. What do you learn from 18:24-19:7 that is relevant to the Body of Christ today? (You might think about one of the optional questions that interests you.)

**For Thought and Discussion:** What did the laying on of hands signify in 19:6? Why did these disciples need the vivid evidence of the Spirit's presence? (Compare 2:4-6, 8:14-17, 10:44-47.)

**For Thought and Discussion:** When the faith spreads quickly, it is common for some "disciples" to get distorted or partial understandings of the gospel. What steps can we take to see that converts understand clearly, and what can we do when we find people confused? (For some examples, see 8:14; 11:22; 14:21-23; 15:36; 18:11,23,26; 19:1-4.)

**Optional Application:** What impresses you about the lifestyle of Paul and the disciples in Ephesus? How can you adopt their attitudes? Ask God for strength and guidance.

**For Thought and Discussion:** Have you ever expected prayer for healing to be effective because you said the right words to God? How is this like attempting magic? How does it dishonor God? Why doesn't prayer for healing work every time, as magic should?

## Power in Ephesus (19:8-22)

***Three months . . . two years*** (19:8,10). The longest Paul spent in any mission city that Luke records. Since Jews reckoned a part of a year as a year, Paul spoke of his time in Ephesus as three years (20:31). During these years, Paul wrote several letters to the church in Corinth, including the one we call 1 Corinthians (1 Corinthians 5:9, 16:8; 2 Corinthians 2:4,9; 7:8-12).

***Lecture hall of Tyrannus*** (19:9). During the normal working hours of morning and evening, Paul earned his keep making tents and leather goods. During the siesta time of 11:00 a.m. to 4:00 p.m., Paul borrowed the building in which someone named Tyrannus taught (or possibly a building this man rented out). Those hot mid-day hours would have been the ones when Tyrannus was not using the building and when working people would have had time to listen to Paul. In a Gentile city, Paul adopted the method of a teacher of philosophy, a role with which his potential audience was familiar.[3]

***Miracles*** (19:11-12). Pagans believed that power emanated from a healer and made even his clothes effective. Apparently God chose to work through that notion, although (as in the case of the bleeding woman, Luke 8:43-48), a person eventually had to face the difference between God's healing power (which He gives as He chooses) and magic (which is an attempt to control and use divine power).

***Chief priest*** (19:14). ***Sceva*** may have been related to the high priestly family, but more probably he used the title to impress people. The Jewish high priest was believed to possess potent secrets, such as the way to pronounce the name of the Jewish God. Charlatans claiming to be magicians and exorcists were all over the Empire (13:6), since people were terrified of Fate and demons and wanted power to deal with them.[4]

***Scrolls*** (19:19). Books were written on scrolls of parchment or papyrus reed. Every town had its sorcerers, astrologers, and exorcists selling their services to cast a spell, mix a love-potion, read a horoscope, or drive out a demon of illness. Ephesus was known as the source of some of the best spells; magical books were known in Greek as "Ephesian letters." ***Fifty thousand drachmas*** was an immense sum for working people—nearly two months' wages for a thousand laborers—but people were willing to spend much hard-earned cash for books that claimed to guarantee health, wealth, power, and happiness.[5]

---

5. From what you know about the people of Ephesus (19:17-20), can you think of a reason why God worked healings and exorcisms through Paul (19:11-12)? If so, explain.

______________________________________

______________________________________

______________________________________

______________________________________

______________________________________

______________________________________

6. Why couldn't Jesus' name be invoked to magically cast out demons (19:13-16)? What else is necessary for the name to be effective?

______________________________________

______________________________________

______________________________________

______________________________________

______________________________________

7. The power of Jesus' name convinced many Ephesians to abandon their vain ways of seeking what they wanted (19:17-19). How is Jesus'

**For Thought and Discussion:** Exactly what is wrong with magic? Why do you think God abhors it so much?

**For Thought and Discussion:** Why was it important for the Ephesians to burn their magical scrolls (19:17-20)? Is there anything you should destroy or get rid of?

**For Thought and Discussion:** How might a Christian use "in Jesus' name" in his prayers with a wrong attitude that approaches magical invocation? How should Acts 19:13-16 help us interpret John 14:13-14?

**For Thought and Discussion:** What good resulted from the miraculous healings in Ephesus?

b. What are some possible drawbacks of a ministry that overemphasizes miracles? How did Paul keep his ministry in balance?

c. How is Jesus' power at work today? Does God use the same methods and do the same things as in Ephesus? Why or why not?

power still at work among us, convincing unbelievers to give up their useless strategies?

## A riot (19:23-41)

Of the dozens of vividly painted temples in Ephesus, the greatest was dedicated to ***Artemis of the Ephesians*** (19:28). It was known as one of the seven wonders of the world:

> 425 feet long, 220 wide, 60 high, with 127 pillars of Parian marble inlaid with gold, and woodwork of cypress and cedar; it was filled with works by the great artists of the Greek world. The priestesses were called bees, and were virgin, the priests or *megabyzi* were eunuchs, drones which 'die' in fertilizing the queen-bee [Artemis]. . . . On 25 May the statues of the goddess were taken up the broad processional road with music, dancing and pageantry to the theatre where they were exhibited to a congregation which might reach 30,000; in Roman times a wealthy Roman paid for a roofed portico to shield the procession from the weather.[6]

All year round, but especially in May, tourists came to see the temple and its rites, and they bought little terra cotta or silver models of the temple as souvenirs (19:24). Ephesian Artemis was a fertility goddess, the Great Mother worshiped in Asia Minor centuries before Rome came. She was not the virgin huntress called Artemis in classical Greek myths. Her image in the temple was a black, squat, many-breasted object of some unknown material. It was said to have fallen from heaven (19:35); the description sounds like a meteorite.[7]

***Craftsmen . . . workmen in related trades*** (19:24-25). Nearly every man in the urban working class belonged to a club with other men in his profession. Although these were social clubs, not political parties, Rome sometimes outlawed them because they encouraged sedition. The smiths or the weavers or the Cretans of a city often rioted when they felt their economic interests threatened, for there was no peaceful, legal means of petitioning the government. Rome left city affairs to local governments for the most part, but ***rioting*** (19:40) was one thing the Romans refused to tolerate and suppressed ruthlessly.[8]

***Officials of the province*** (19:31). The *Asiarchs* were the aristocratic rulers of Ephesus who represented the city in the council of confederated cities of Asia.[9] An Asiarch could also be an aristocrat elected to preside over the emperor cult in his city—this was a half-religious, half-political job of promoting patriotism.[10] Paul had friends in high places.

***Crowd . . . assembly*** (19:30,32,39,41). The *demos* or *ekklesia* was the citizens' assembly that met three times a month in the theater to decide certain cases.[11] However, this gathering of the *demos* was behaving more like a mob (the Greek is *ochlos*, "mob," in 19:33,35) than a legal body.

***City clerk*** (19:35). He was the chief executive officer of Ephesus. He published the decisions of the citizens' assembly, received official correspondence, and acted as liason between the city and the Roman provincial government.[12] If there was a riot in Ephesus, Rome would hold him and the Asiarchs responsible.

8. Why were the Ephesian silversmiths against Paul (19:23-27)?

______________________________

______________________________

______________________________

**For Thought and Discussion:** How do people you know attempt to gain health, money, love, success, and security? Are any of their methods similar to magic? (Think about the health books, money books, or success books you have seen.)

**For Thought and Discussion:** Is healing still one way God shows His power? What are some other ways?

**For Thought and Discussion:** a. Why do you think the gospel so often conflicts with people's economic interests? What kinds of businesses does it threaten?

b. How should Christians deal with people whose livelihoods are threatened by the gospel?

9. How was this reason similar to the one that set some Philippians against Paul and Silas (16:16-21)?

10. Do economic interests set any groups against the gospel today? If so, give an example.

11. What protected Paul from the violence of an outraged mob (19:31,35-41)?

12. In light of this episode (19:37-40) and the one in Corinth (18:12-17), explain why Paul and Peter considered it so important that Christians carefully obey the civil laws (Romans 13:1-7, 1 Peter 2:13-17).

13. How is this episode relevant to your life? (What does it reveal about the Church in the world? What attitudes and habits does it encourage you to adopt?)

14. What one insight from 18:24-19:41 would you like to focus on for application this week? How do you want to be changed by this insight?

15. With what prayer and/or action will you begin addressing this area, with God's help?

16. Note any thoughts you have on the topics on pages 32-34.

**For Thought and Discussion:** What does 19:23-41 contribute to the story of Acts as a whole? How does it reflect the themes of Acts?

**For Further Study:** Add 18:24-19:41 to your outline.

17. List any questions you have about 18:24-19:41.

______________________________

______________________________

______________________________

## For the group

**Warm-up.** Ask, "What aspects of your former lifestyle did you have to give up when you became serious about being a Christian?" This may help the group identify with the Ephesians who had to give up magic, profits from religious tourism, and the pleasures of the pagan temples.

**Ephesus.** As before, you may have to focus on one or two of the episodes that seem relevant to the group.

**Worship.** Thank God for baptizing you into Jesus and giving you the Holy Spirit. Praise God for His power over magic and victory over illness, evil spirits, and ungodly economic interests. Pray for new converts and those who train them, asking that they might all clearly understand and explain the gospel.

1. Helmut Koester, *Introduction to the New Testament: Volume 2: History and Literature of Earliest Christianity* (Philadelphia: Fortress Press, 1982), pages 219-220.
2. Marshall, pages 305-306.
3. Marshall, page 309.
4. Ferguson, pages 77-87, 153-189; Koester, *Introduction to the New Testament: Volume 1: History, Culture, and Literature of the Hellenistic World,* pages 156-159, 376-381; Bruce, *Paul,* page 292.
5. Bruce, *Paul,* page 291; Kent, page 152.
6. Ferguson, page 21.
7. Barclay, page 141; *The NIV Study Bible,* page 1684. According to Kent, page 153, the image of Artemis looked like a woman with many breasts and may have been made from a meteorite. See also plate 6 in Ferguson.
8. Bruce, *Paul,* page 294.
9. Bruce, *Paul,* page 288.
10. Marshall, page 319; Kent, page 154.
11. Bruce, *Paul,* page 294; Marshall, pages 318-319; *The NIV Study Bible,* page 1685.
12. Bruce, *Paul,* page 288; *The NIV Study Bible,* page 1685; Marshall, pages 319-320.

LESSON SIXTEEN

# ACTS 20:1-21:16

## Paul's Farewells

Even before the silversmiths' riot, Paul had planned to leave Ephesus and go to Jerusalem (19:21). Although Luke barely mentions the reason (24:17), we know that Paul's chief errand was to deliver money collected from his Gentile churches as a gift to the poor believers in Jerusalem (Romans 15:25-33, 1 Corinthians 16:1-4, 2 Corinthians 8:1-9:15). To gather this money, Paul intended to visit the churches in Macedonia and Achaia—in Philippi, Thessalonica, Berea, and Corinth.

From Acts 19:21 and Romans 1:8-15, 15:17-33, we also know that Paul was already convinced he "must visit Rome also" and that he hoped to bring the gospel to Spain thereafter. Thus, he already planned his visits with the disciples of Macedonia, Corinth, Troas, and Ephesus to be goodbyes as well as pastoral sessions. However, something told those who were spiritually sensitive that this might be a more serious farewell than they hoped. As you read 20:1-21:16, watch for signs of the bond of fellowship among the believers.

### Macedonia and Greece (20:1-6)

Luke tells us little of what Paul did after he left Ephesus and before he reached Greece (20:2), but Paul's letters fill in some details. While in Ephesus, Paul learned of a dispute in the Corinthian church. He sent two letters to settle the strife (one is lost; the other is 1 Corinthians), but neither the letters nor a visit by Timothy (1 Corinthians 4:17) achieved peace. Paul even went to Corinth briefly himself, but he was humiliated by the defiant factions; Paul called that visit "painful" (2 Corinthians 2:1). Back in Ephesus, Paul wrote a severe letter "out of great distress and anguish of heart" (2 Corinthians 2:3-4). That letter he sent by the hand of Titus, another of his young associates (like Timothy, but perhaps a more forceful personality). This anguished letter is also lost.

All this happened before Paul left Ephesus. Now, as he ***set out for Macedonia*** (Acts 20:1), he went first to Troas, hoping to meet Titus on his way back from Corinth with a response. Paul did some successful evangelism in Troas, but when Titus did not arrive, the apostle went on to Macedonia (2 Corinthians 2:12-13). There Titus met him with good news: the Corinthians had repented of their rebellion. Paul quickly sent Titus back with a fourth letter full of affection—our 2 Corinthians.[1]

Now that there was peace, Paul was free to visit Corinth after Macedonia. The ***three months*** (20:3) he spent in ***Greece*** (20:2) were probably a winter in Corinth while travel was difficult. Paul probably used this time to compose his letter to the Romans.[2]

***He was accompanied by*** (20:4). These were representatives of each church that had given money for Jerusalem; they were going to accompany Paul with the gift. No delegate from Philippi is mentioned, but Luke apparently joined the party at Philippi (notice the "we" in 20:6).

***Feast of Unleavened Bread*** (20:6). The eight-day Jewish festival that began with Passover. Marshall thinks Paul "was celebrating the Christian Passover, *i.e.* Easter, with the church at Philippi (1 Corinthians 5:7-8)."[3]

## Miracle in Troas (20:7-12)

***Break bread*** (20:7). The meeting probably included both the Lord's Supper and the Agape, the love feast that Christians commonly held along with the Lord's Supper (1 Corinthians 11:17-34 discusses the same double observance).[4]

***In a window*** (20:9). Lower class people in Roman towns often lived in multi-story tenements. The large windows had no glass panes. The stuffiness, the smell of the oil ***lamps*** (20:8), and the incessant talking was too much for one ***young man***—the Greek word indicates a boy between eight and fourteen.[5]

---

1. In the events of 20:1-21:16, how did the various believers show fellowship/partnership/communion with each other? What feelings did they express, and how?

20:1-6 ______________________________

______________________________

______________________________

______________________________

______________________________

______________________________

20:7-12 ______________________________

______________________________

______________________________

______________________________

______________________________

______________________________

20:13-38 ______________________________

______________________________

______________________________

______________________________

______________________________

______________________________

21:1-16 ___________________________________

___________________________________

___________________________________

___________________________________

___________________________________

___________________________________

___________________________________

2. What good examples do you see here for the way churches should function and the way believers should treat and feel about each other?

___________________________________

___________________________________

___________________________________

___________________________________

___________________________________

___________________________________

___________________________________

## Farewell to the Ephesian elders
(20:13-38)

***Assos*** (20:13). While Paul walked twenty miles south from Troas, the others sailed forty miles around the peninsula, so they all arrived at Assos at about the same time. They then continued down the coast of Asia, stopping at night at ***Mitylene*** (20:14) on the isle of Lesbos, on ***Kios*** (20:15), on ***Samos***, and finally at ***Miletus***. There the ship planned to stop for a day or two, so Paul summoned the elders from Ephesus, thirty miles north, to bid him farewell.

***Pentecost*** (20:16). Of the fifty days between Passover and Pentecost, sixteen had passed (20:6,13-15). If Paul had stopped at Ephesus, he would have had to visit many families and change ships, and there might even have been trouble from local enemies. All that would have taken more time than Paul could afford.

Observant Jews tried to be in Jerusalem for either Passover or Pentecost as often as possible. We don't know why this Pentecost was important to Paul; he may have wanted to bring the gift of money in time for the occasion, or he may have wanted to celebrate his ancestral customs even though Christ had given them new meaning.

**For Thought and Discussion:** What can 20:18-37 teach us about how Christian leaders should think and act? How can you help the leaders in your church to practice this example?

3. What actions and attitudes had Paul practiced as a model for Christian leaders (20:17-27,33-35)?

4. What warning and command did Paul repeat (20:28-31)?

5. What would protect the elders in the face of this danger (20:32)?

**For Thought and Discussion:** Paul and the other believers agreed that the Holy Spirit promised suffering if Paul went to Jerusalem, but they differed as to what the Spirit wanted Paul to do in light of the warning (20:22-25; 21:4,10-13). Why do we often interpret the Spirit's guidance differently? What should we do in such situations? (In your opinion, what should Paul and the others have done in 21:12-14?)

## To Jerusalem (21:1-16)

***Cos . . . Rhodes . . . Patara*** (21:1). See the map on page 20.

***Phoenicia*** (21:2). A coastal district of the province of ***Syria*** (21:3). Phoenicia's chief city was the port of ***Tyre*** (21:3). ***Ptolemais*** (21:7) was a day's sailing further south, and ***Caesarea*** (21:8) was a day further.

***Philip the evangelist*** (21:8). About twenty-five years earlier, Philip reached Caesarea on his missionary wanderings (8:40). Apparently, he eventually settled there, married, and raised a family. "Evangelist" may have been Philip's office, as Paul was an apostle and Agabus was a prophet.

***Agabus*** (21:10). The same man who prophesied famine about fifteen years earlier (11:27-29). His demonstrative method of prophecy (21:11) was used by Old Testament prophets to make their points more vivid that mere words could.

6. Why was Paul going to Jerusalem (20:22, 24:17)?

______________________________

______________________________

______________________________

______________________________

7. The Holy Spirit repeatedly warned Paul both internally and through prophets that danger waited in Jerusalem (20:22-25; 21:4,10-13). With what attitude did Paul respond to these warnings (20:24, 21:13)?

______________________________

______________________________

______________________________

______________________________

8. Why do you think the Holy Spirit warned Paul repeatedly of his destiny in Jerusalem? (For instance, did He want Paul not to go? Why do you think so or not?)

______________________________________

______________________________________

______________________________________

______________________________________

______________________________________

9. What does 20:1-21:16 reveal about God, especially the Holy Spirit?

______________________________________

______________________________________

______________________________________

______________________________________

10. What insight from 20:1-21:16 would you like to concentrate on for application this week? How do you want to grow or obey in this area?

______________________________________

______________________________________

______________________________________

______________________________________

______________________________________

11. What steps do you plan to take to begin applying this truth?

______________________________________

______________________________________

______________________________________

______________________________________

______________________________________

**For Thought and Discussion:** In your judgment, was Paul right or wrong to go to Jerusalem? Why?

**Optional Application:** Are you disagreeing with other believers about the Spirit's will in some area? What should you do?

**For Further Study:** Add 20:1-21:16 to your outline.

12. On pages 32-34, record what you learned from 20:1-21:16 about the topics there.

13. List any questions you have about 20:1-21:16.

______________________________

______________________________

______________________________

______________________________

## For the group

**Warm-up.** Ask, "Have you ever disagreed with other Christians about what the Spirit was guiding you to do? If so, what were the circumstances, and how did you decide what was right?"

**Questions.** Acts 20:1-21:16 records some good examples for churches and leaders. List and explain as many as you can. Then ask how any of those apply to your group or church. What aspects of 20:1-21:16 are norms you must follow, which ones are models you may follow, and which are unique to the first-century situation? How can you decide?

**Worship.** Thank God for making Christians into one Body and inspiring the kind of love the believers in Troas, Ephesus, and elsewhere felt for Paul and each other. Ask God to give you that kind of love for fellow Christians. Thank Him for the Holy Spirit, and ask for the wisdom to interpret His guidance accurately.

1. Bruce, *Paul,* pages 264, 273-276, 317-318; Marshall, page 322.
2. Marshall, page 323.
3. Marshall, page 325.
4. Marshall, page 326; Barclay, page 149.
5. Marshall, page 327; Barclay, page 149.

LESSON SEVENTEEN

# ACTS 21:17-23:11

## Arrest in Jerusalem

Just as Jesus set his face to go to Jerusalem, knowing He would die there (Luke 9:21-22,44,51), so Paul went resolutely to the Holy City, prepared for the same fate (Acts 21:13). A new generation of Jews and Romans controlled the land since Jesus' death, but Paul knew that the passions which moved him to approve the stoning of Stephen still burned in his countrymen. He had so much in common with his Jewish brethren that his heart ached to draw them across the gulf which now separated them (Romans 9:1-5, 10:1, 11:13-16). As you read Acts 21:17-23:11, try to feel what Paul felt when he faced his people.

### Agreement with the elders (21:17-26)

***James . . . the elders*** (21:18). Now that the twelve apostles were scattered on missionary trips, these men led the church in Jerusalem. Paul was staying with Mnason, a Hellenistic Jewish Christian[1] (21:16), but now he met with the Hebraic Christian leaders. Luke emphasizes the report of the Gentile mission at this meeting (21:19), but this was also probably the moment when Paul and the Gentile delegates presented their gift of charity. Luke doesn't say how the Jewish believers felt about receiving the money from Gentiles; Paul had earlier expressed some concern about this (Romans 15:31).

**For Thought and Discussion:** a. In your judgment, did the request for Paul to pay for the Nazirites undermine the agreement mentioned in 21:25? Why or why not?

b. By joining in Jewish rites, do you think Paul was undermining his teaching to the Gentiles in Galatians 2:11-5:15? Was he being like Peter in Galatians 2:11-14? Why or why not? (You might look at Romans 15:1-2, 1 Corinthians 9:19-23.)

c. Was Paul right or wrong to participate in the purification and the Nazirite vows? What scriptural principles determine your opinion?

***Turn away from Moses*** (21:21). These rumors were false, but we can understand how they arose. Paul did teach Gentiles not to keep the Law, but he insisted that Jewish believers were free to maintain their customs (Romans 14:1-15:13). He himself had circumcised Timothy because the lad was a Jew and had taken a Nazirite vow (Acts 16:3, 18:18). However, Paul's own freedom among the Gentiles (1 Corinthians 9:19-23), his teaching that law-keeping did not enhance a Jewish believer's standing before God (Romans 2:25-29, Galatians 5:6), and his disparaging comments about the Law (Galatians 4:9) might have led some of his Jewish converts to give up their customs without Paul telling them to do so.[2]

***Purification rites*** (21:24). If a person under a Nazirite vow touched a dead body, he became ritually unclean. He then had to offer animal sacrifices to cleanse himself before he could complete his vow (Numbers 6:9-12). Paul knew that Jesus was the eternal sin offering (Romans 8:3) and that baptism into Jesus made a person permanently clean, but he apparently felt that performing ritual cleansing did not contradict faith in the grace of Jesus' sacrifice. Paul evidently regarded the Nazirite rite as an acceptable custom for Jews, although he would not have approved of Gentiles performing Jewish rituals.

***Expenses*** (21:24). Numbers 6:9-21 suggests how expensive the offerings of animals, bread, and wine would have been. It was considered an act of piety for someone with wealth to pay for a poorer man's vow of gratitude to God; King Agrippa I did so often.[3]

---

1. Why did the leaders of the Jerusalem church want Paul to participate in the vow (21:20-25)? In their eyes, how would this act serve the gospel?

______________________________________

______________________________________

2. What might have been some of Paul's reasons for doing as these believers asked? (Do 1 Corinthians 9:19-23 and Romans 14:13-15:3 shed light on his possible motives?)

3. What can 21:17-26 teach us about dealing with differences within the Church today?

## Arrest (21:27-39)

***Brought Greeks*** (21:28). The outer court of the Temple was called the Court of the Gentiles. At the gate from that one to the inner courts was a low barrier and a sign warning that any Gentile who entered had himself to blame when he was instantly killed. The Romans permitted this death sentence just as they upheld the holiness of other religions' sanctuaries. However, it is highly unlikely that Paul did bring a Gentile into the inner Temple, especially since his accusers did not seize the alleged Gentile.[4]

**Optional Application:** Are you called upon to weigh Christian fellowship against personal beliefs about what should be done? If so, what should you choose? (Talk to God about this.)

**Optional Application:** How might a modern missionary face a conflict between customs in his home church and freedom in his mission field?

**Optional Application:** What ethnic or religious customs (Jewish, Catholic, American, African, etc.) may a believer practice, and what customs may he not practice? (Think of some specific examples that are important to you.) How do you decide?

**For Further Study:** How were the accusations against Paul like and unlike those against Stephen (6:11-14, 21:27-28)? Why is this significant?

**For Thought and Discussion:** In 22:1-21, why do you suppose Paul didn't defend himself against the charge of defiling the temple (21:28)? What was the real issue at stake?

***Commander*** (21:31). The tribune of a cohort (about a thousand troops). These were stationed in the Antonia Fortress beside the Temple.[5] The cohort was charged with keeping order in Jerusalem, where hatred of Rome was seething, murders were increasingly frequent, and riot might explode at any moment.

***The Egyptian who started a revolt*** (21:38). Josephus wrote that an Egyptian false prophet "led 30,000 men to the Mount of Olives in order to take Jerusalem"[6] (Josephus tended to exaggerate numbers). His followers were all killed, but the leader escaped. The Roman tribune assumed that Paul was this man back in town.

The Egyptian's followers were called *sicarii* (***terrorists***; "assassins" in RSV) because they used a short dagger, called a *sica* in Latin, to assassinate powerful Jews who collaborated with Rome. These *sicarii* eventually led the disastrous revolt against Rome in 66-70 AD, and even now in 57 AD they were considered highly dangerous.[7]

## **Paul's defense to the Jews** (21:40-22:29)

***Aramaic*** (21:40, 22:2). The Greek word could mean Hebrew (NASB, KJV), but Aramaic was the common language of the people. The two languages were related, so the people could have understood Hebrew with some effort (like modern people hearing a man speak King James English). Because many Jews outside Palestine could not speak Aramaic or Hebrew, Paul was identifying himself with his audience of patriotic, conservative Palestinian Jews by using their ancestral tongue.[8]

***Witness . . . martyr*** (22:15, 20). The Greek word *martys* meant "witness," but in Christian circles it gained the sense of "witness unto death" because of what so often happened to witnesses for Christ.

4. Paul called his speech a "defense" (22:1; Greek·

*apologia*). Summarize what he said to the Jews in 22:1-21.

______________________________________

______________________________________

______________________________________

______________________________________

______________________________________

______________________________________

5. How did Paul shape this speech to appeal to the Jews? Observe the details in 21:40-22:21.

______________________________________

______________________________________

______________________________________

______________________________________

______________________________________

6. Why did 22:21 make the Jews interrupt with rage?

______________________________________

______________________________________

______________________________________

______________________________________

7. What might make people of your country react as in 22:22 to an evangelist? What aspects of the gospel seem offensive or unethical to your people?

______________________________________

______________________________________

______________________________________

______________________________________

______________________________________

**Optional Application:** For what three important things had God chosen Paul (22:14)? To what extent have you been chosen for these? How should you respond?

**Optional Application:** What would you say in your country if you had a chance to give a "defense" as Paul did? Plan out some of the things you could say.

**For Thought and Discussion:** a. What do you think was the purpose of the promise in 23:11? What does it tell you about the Lord?

b. Does He ever do things like this for you? Do you know why or why not?

8. Paul might have known that 22:21 would infuriate the Jews. Why do you think he risked his life to say 22:6-21, instead of just refuting the charge of defiling the Temple?

______________________________

______________________________

______________________________

______________________________

______________________________

***Flogged*** (22:24). The tribune could not comprehend Paul's speech in Aramaic, full of religious terms, so he decided to have Paul tortured for the straight story. The *scourge* was a bundle of leather whips with pieces of lead or bone fixed to the ends. Scourging was far worse than a Jewish beating or the Roman beating with rods (16:22); victims often died from it. Therefore, it was legal to scourge slaves and non-Romans, but it was expressly forbidden to scourge a ***Roman citizen*** (22:25).[9]

Roman citizenship was not very easy to obtain in Paul's day. A person could 1) receive it as a reward for military or other service to Rome; 2) receive it when freed from slavery to a citizen; 3) bribe key Roman officials; or 4) be born into a family of citizens. The fourth was the most prestigious way.[10]

## Before the Sanhedrin (22:30-23:11)

Since the tribune couldn't torture Paul to learn his crime, he summoned the Sanhedrin to hear Paul and explain why he was offensive to the Jews.

***Ananias*** (23:2). He was high priest from 47 to 59 AD, then assassinated by the *sicarii* as a Roman pawn in 66 AD. Josephus agrees that Ananias was "insolent and quick-tempered."[11]

***Whitewashed wall*** (23:3). A hypocrite: either a tomb whitewashed to mark its unclean interior (Matthew 23:27) or a flimsy wall whitewashed to appear firm (Ezekiel 13:10-12).[12] Paul may have lost his temper (compare Matthew 5:39, 1 Corinthians 4:12), or he may have been pronouncing a solemn curse by God's prompting. The *sicarii's* dagger was an effective fulfillment of this promise.

***I did not realize that he was the high priest*** (23:5). Although many explanations for this extraordinary statement have been offered, including that Paul had poor eyesight or that Ananias was dressed in ordinary clothes, most modern commentators find it unlikely that Paul did not recognize the high priest. His words were ironical: "I did not think that a man who could give such an order could be the high priest."[13]

---

9. What does 21:16-23:11 contribute to the overall message of the book?

_______________

_______________

_______________

_______________

_______________

10. What one truth from these passages would you like to take to heart this week? How can you apply it?

_______________

_______________

_______________

_______________

_______________

11. On pages 32-34, write what 21:16-23:11 tells you about those topics.

**For Thought and Discussion:** In what sense was the division between the Pharisees and Sadducees (see the notes on pages 56-57) at the heart of the issue for which Paul was on trial—the issue of whether Christianity was the true fulfillment of Judaism?

**For Thought and Discussion:** What was God's role in the events of 21:16-23:11?

**For Further Study:** Add 21:16-23:11 to your outline.

12. List any questions you have about this lesson.

______________________________

______________________________

______________________________

______________________________

## For the group

**Warm-up.** Ask whether anyone has had a chance to witness to his or her faith since beginning this study of Acts. If so, ask what happened.

**Agreement with the elders.** You may have quite a debate over whether or not Paul should have participated in Jewish rituals connected with the Temple. Try to help the group see why the Jerusalem Christians felt this was both an important and a Christian thing to do. Then examine reasons why Paul should or shouldn't have obliged the elders. How might a modern Christian be faced with a similar decision?

**Paul's defense.**

**Worship.** Praise God for showing His witnesses what to say when they are called upon to make a defense. Ask God to give you wisdom and courage for the mission He has given you.

1. Mnason had a Greek name and came from Cyprus.
2. Marshall, page 344; Kent, page 162.
3. Kent, page 162.
4. Marshall, pages 347-348; Kent, pages 163-164.
5. Marshall, page 348.
6. Marshall, page 351; Josephus, *The Jewish War,* book 2, chapters 261-263.
7. Bruce, *New Testament History,* pages 98-99, 339-340; Marshall, pages 351-352.
8. Marshall, pages 352-353.
9. *The NIV Study Bible,* page 1690; Marshall, pages 358-359.
10. *The NIV Study Bible,* page 1690; Marshall, page 359; John J. O'Rourke, "Roman Law and the Early Church," *The Catacombs and the Colosseum,* pages 176-177.
11. Marshall, page 363, citing Josephus, *Antiquities,* chapter 199.
12. Marshall, page 363.
13. Marshall, pages 363-364. See Barclay, pages 164-165; Kent, page 168.

LESSON EIGHTEEN

# ACTS 23:11-26:32

## Prisoner in Caesarea

On the day of Paul's baptism, the Lord had said of him, "This man is my chosen instrument to carry my name before the Gentiles and their kings and before the people of Israel. I will show him how much he must suffer for my name" (9:15-16). Paul's mission was to be a witness for the Righteous One (22:14-15), to testify to the gospel of God's grace (20:24). In God's eyes, these years in prison were as crucial to His plan as the years in Corinth and Ephesus.

Before you begin this lesson, read Luke 12:8-12 and 21:12-19. Then read Acts 23:11-26:32 prayerfully, observing how Paul acted before governors and kings and imagining yourself in his place.

**For Thought and Discussion:** How do Luke 12:8-12 and 21:12-19 resemble Paul's experiences and actions?

1. The Lord discloses His plan in 23:11. How do this verse and 9:15-16 summarize what happens in the following sections of Acts?

   21:17-23:10 ______________________________

   ______________________________

   ______________________________

   ______________________________

   23:12-26:32 ______________________________

   ______________________________

   ______________________________

   ______________________________

**For Thought and Discussion:** How does the oath of 23:12 reflect a different attitude toward God than the Nazirite vow?

27:1-28:31 ______________________________

______________________________

______________________________

______________________________

## A plot thwarted (23:12-35)

***Oath*** (23:12). Unlike the Nazirite vow of dedication and gratitude, this was a vow called *cherem* in which a person invoked God to curse him if he broke the vow. Jewish law did, however, provide loopholes for escaping the curse if one failed to keep the oath. The conspirators were probably members of the Zealots or the *sicarii*, the extremist patriots or terrorists who later led the Jewish revolt in 66-70 AD (see the note to 21:38 on page 182). These groups assassinated many people whom they considered threats to the true religion of God.[1]

***No charge against him that deserved death*** (23:29). The charge of defiling the Temple was apparently dropped for lack of evidence, although it turned up again (24:6). Commander Lysias' judgment is important: if Paul was later executed, it was not because he had broken any law, but because he had angered the Jews and fell victim to Roman politics.[2]

***Antipatris*** (23:31). A military post thirty-seven miles from Jerusalem and twenty-five from Caesarea.[3]

***From Cilicia*** (23:34). Cases were usually tried in the province where the alleged crime was committed, but a governor could foist a touchy case onto the prisoner's home province. However, Governor Felix knew the Sanhedrin would not appreciate traveling to Cilicia for the trial and the legate of Syria would not appreciate being handed a silly case.[4]

***Herod's palace*** (23:35). Herod the Great had built it, but now it was used as a *praetorium*—"the headquarters of the Roman administration."[5]

Paul's letter to the Philippians was written from a *praetorium* either in Caesarea or Rome (Philippians 1:13).

2. Consider the lengths to which the Jewish fanatics were willing to go to silence Paul (23:12-15). What human and divine factors prevented them (23:16-30)?

**For Thought and Discussion:** Compare Paul's introduction (24:10) to Tertullus's (24:2-3). How are they different, and why?

## Trial before Felix (24:1-27)

***Felix*** (23:26, 24:2). He was born a slave, but because his brother Pallas was "a corrupt favorite"[6] of the emperors Claudius and Nero, Felix was first freed and later promoted. He became "the first slave in history ever to become governor of a Roman province";[7] this office was usually reserved for Roman knights. (The reigns of Claudius and Nero were notorious for allowing freedmen to virtually run the Empire.)

Felix became governor of Judea in 52 AD but was recalled in 59 AD for mishandling riots, overusing violence, and other acts of incompetence and corruption.[8] The Roman historian Tacitus summarized Felix's character thus: "He exercised the prerogatives of a king with the spirit of a slave."[9]

***Peace . . . foresight . . . reforms . . . gratitude*** (24:2-3). It was customary to begin by flattering the magistrate to gain his favor, and Tertullus did not mind stretching the truth. In fact, there were frequent riots during Felix's tenure, and the Jews detested him for his methods and manners.[10]

**For Thought and Discussion:** a. Why was it so important to Paul to keep a clear conscience before God and man (23:1, 24:16)?

b. Is this important to you? If so, why? How do you show it?

**For Thought and Discussion:** Describe the attitudes and emotions Paul seemed to have as he defended himself. What do you learn about him that is worthy of imitation?

**Optional Application:** a. What do you think were the truths about righteousness, self-control, and judgment that Paul discoursed upon (24:25)?

b. How should these truths affect your attitudes and actions? How are these relevant to the decisions currently facing you? Talk to God about this.

***Troublemaker*** (24:5). Literally, "pestilence." To incite dissension was treason against the emperor.

***Ringleader of the Nazarene sect*** (24:5). Tertullus claimed that Christianity (Jesus of Nazareth was called a Nazarene) was not a branch of Judaism but a cult not approved by Rome. The Romans were conservative polytheists: they were happy to let subject peoples worship their ancestral gods (see Paul's claim in 24:14), but they disliked "new" religions.[11] Tertullus needed to prove that the Way was not Judaism, and Paul needed to prove that it was true Judaism.

---

3. How did Paul refute each of Tertullus's charges against him?

making trouble, inciting dissension (24:11-13,17-18)

______________________________

______________________________

______________________________

______________________________

leading a new and unlawful sect (24:14-16)

______________________________

______________________________

______________________________

______________________________

______________________________

desecrating the Temple (24:11-13,17-21)

______________________________

______________________________

______________________________

______________________________

4. Why is it important to us that Paul claimed Christianity was not something new, but the true continuation of the faith recorded in the Law and the Prophets?

---

*Drusilla* (24:24). Felix's third wife. When she was sixteen, Felix used a magician to persuade her to leave her first husband for him.[12]

---

5. a. How did his expectation of resurrection and possible judgment affect Paul (24:15-16)?

b. How did this idea affect Felix (24:25)?

c. Why do you think the prospect of judgment affected these men so differently?

**For Further Study:** On the resurrection of the just and unjust (24:15), see Matthew 25:31-46, John 5:28-30, Romans 2:5-8, 2 Corinthians 5:10, 1 Thessalonians 4:14-17.

**For Thought and Discussion:** "Self-control" (24:25) was one of the highest virtues according to Stoic philosophers, so aristocrats paid lip service to it. Paul used a term tht Felix knew and had to profess to believe in, but he put it into a Christian context. What are some virtues and values that people in your culture pay lip service to? How can you use them in explaining the gospel?

**Optional Application:** Put yourself in Paul's place in 24:23-26. Would you have tried to raise money to buy your way out of prison, or would you have preached to Felix? What does this tell you about Paul and yourself?

**For Thought and Discussion:** Paul allowed Jason to pay bond to release him from jail (17:9), but he refused to pay a bribe to be released by Felix (24:26). Why do you think the first was acceptable but the last was not?

**For Further Study:** On Paul's view of the Law (Acts 25:8) see Romans 7:12, 8:3-4; 1 Corinthians 9:20. On his attitude toward Caesar, see Romans 13:1-7, 1 Timothy 2:2.

**For Thought and Discussion:** In your judgment, should Paul have appealed to Caesar or trusted God to protect him in Jerusalem? Why?

***Porcius Festus*** (24:27). According to Josephus, he was much more prudent and honest than Felix, but he died after just two years in office.[13]

***Grant a favor to the Jews*** (24:27). Felix was going to Rome to face Jewish accusations of gross mishandling of a mob in Caesarea.[14] He hoped that by leaving Paul in prison he might avoid even more anger from the Jews.

## Festus (25:1-12)

***Are you willing to go up to Jerusalem . . . ?*** (25:9). A question like this from a governor was effectively a decision.[15] In Jerusalem, members of the Sanhedrin would be on Festus's official board of advisors (see 25:12) and could even engineer evidence and public outcry against Paul.

***I appeal to Caesar!*** (25:11). If a Roman citizen had not broken a specific statute, he had the right to appeal for a trial before the emperor.[16] An acquittal in Rome might protect Christians from prosecution for decades, and Paul would have loved the chance to declare the gospel to the emperor himself. (Paul had no way of knowing it, but Nero usually delegated cases to other judges rather than sit through such tiresome business himself.[17])

Paul did not fear death (25:11), but there was no sense in throwing his life away in Jerusalem when he might accomplish so much through a trial in Rome.

6. Lysias, Felix, and Festus all knew that Paul had broken no Roman laws (23:29, 24:22-27, 25:18-20). Why didn't they free him?

______________________________

______________________________

______________________________

______________________________

## Agrippa (25:13-26:32)

Having appealed to Rome, Paul could not now be tried by Festus or his colleague Agrippa. But Festus could ask a well-informed neighboring king to advise him about what to write in the legal brief he had to send with Paul to Rome.

---

***Agrippa*** (25:13). Herod Agrippa II, the son of Herod Agrippa I who died in 44 BC (12:23). Agrippa II ruled some territory in northeast Palestine and tried constantly to make peace between the Jews and Rome. As official head of Judaism (Agrippa had the right to appoint the high priest, controlled who had the priest's sacred vestments, etc.), he was the logical man to advise Festus on a case like Paul's.

After the death of her husband, Agrippa's sister ***Bernice*** moved in with him; there were rumors of incest. Later, she became mistress to Emperor Vespasian and then Emperor Titus.[18]

---

7. What did Paul think was the issue for which he was being held prisoner (26:6-8)?

________________________________________

________________________________________

________________________________________

________________________________________

8. Summarize the gist of what Paul said to Agrippa (26:2-23).

________________________________________

________________________________________

________________________________________

________________________________________

________________________________________

________________________________________

**For Thought and Discussion:** Why do you suppose God put the gospel at the mercy of people like Felix, Agrippa I, and Agrippa II? What does this tell you about God? Does He still do this today?

**For Thought and Discussion:** Why do you think Paul so often told about his conversion in his defenses (22:2-21, 26:2-23)? Why was this a good evangelistic technique?

**Optional Application:** a. If you had a chance to proclaim your faith to a high official, what would you say? Pray and plan out a possible speech. Would you say anything about your past and how Christ changed you? If so, what?

b. Ask God to send you someone to whom you can tell these things or some other words He gives to you.

**Optional Application:** Meditate on 26:16-18 this week. What difference do these truths make to your life, your actions, and your attitudes?

**For Thought and Discussion:** Why was the Resurrection the decisive issue between Paul and the Jews? Is it the decisive issue between you and anyone? Why or why not?

**Optional Application:** In 26:17-18, Jesus tells what He will do for people. What must they do in response (26:20)? How can you prove your repentance by your deeds this week?

9. Agrippa could do nothing to free Paul since he had appealed to Caesar. Why did Paul gave this speech and the words in 26:25-27? (See 26:29.)

10. How does Paul set an example for you as a Christian in 23:12-26:32? (Consider especially 24:10-26, 25:8-11, 26:1-29.)

11. What overall impression of the Roman system do you get from 23:12-26:32? Summarize both the good and the bad points.

12. What one aspect of Paul's example or another insight from 23:12-26:32 would you like to apply?

13. Describe some specific steps you can take to let this insight influence your habits and character.

14. Record any observations you would like to make regarding the topics on pages 32-34.

15. List any questions you have about 23:12-26:32.

## For the group

**Warm-up.** Ask, "During the past week, has your expectation of resurrection and judgment made any difference to your thoughts or actions? If so, how? If not, why not?"

**Read and summarize.** Question 1 gives you a quick overview of the rest of Acts: Paul testifies in Jerusalem and before kings, is sent to Rome, and finally testifies in Rome. All this was the fulfillment of God's stated intentions.

**Questions.** You may want to focus on just one or two of the issues in this lesson: the relationship between Judaism and Christianity (questions 3 and 4), resurrection and judgment (question 5), or how

**For Thought and Discussion:** In your judgment, does this section of Acts in any way illustrate what a Christian should expect from a governmental system and how he or she should deal with it? If so, explain.

**Optional Application:** How did Jesus change Paul's life and character (26:2-23)? How has He changed yours? What should you do about these facts?

**For Thought and Discussion:** Why do you think Luke was so interested in detailing the relationship between Christianity and the government (the Sanhedrin; the Philippian and Thessalonian magistrates; the governors Sergius Paulus, Gallio, Felix, and Festus; and King Agrippa)?

Paul dealt with civil authorities (questions 6-9). Or, use question 10 as a springboard to find out what interested group members.

Question 4 is a deep issue that the group may not have thought about before. If necessary, suggest some possible answers to get the discussion going. For instance, the Old Testament tells us what God is like and what He expects of us. It gives our beliefs historical roots: Jesus did not enter the world in a historical vacuum; instead, the Old Testament helps to explain Him. Christians claim the same covenant relationship with the same God that the Old Testament Israelites knew.

If your group is not interested in the relationship between Christianity and the government, briefly discuss why this matter was so important to Luke. Then you can skip this topic if you have covered it in a previous lesson.

**Worship.** Praise God for giving His witnesses words to speak before kings and governors. Thank Him for the promised Resurrection and Judgment. Ask God to help you develop righteousness, self-control, and a clear conscience.

1. Marshall, page 367; Barclay, page 166.
2. Marshall, pages 371-372.
3. Marshall, page 372; *The NIV Study Bible,* page 1692 says Antipatris was thirty miles from Jerusalem and twenty-eight from Caesarea—perhaps by slightly different routes.
4. Marshall, page 373.
5. Marshall, page 373.
6. Marshall, page 370.
7. Barclay, pages 167-168.
8. Marshall, page 370; *The NIV Study Bible,* page 1693.
9. Barclay, page 168.
10. Marshall, page 374; *The NIV Study Bible,* page 1692.
11. Ramsay MacMullen, *Paganism in the Roman Empire* (New Haven: Yale University Press, 1981), pages 2-4; Koester, *Introduction to the New Testament: Volume 1: History, Culture, and Literature of the Hellenistic World,* pages 362-366.
12. *The NIV Study Bible,* page 1693; Marshall, page 381.
13. Josephus, *The Jewish War,* book 2, chapter 14; *Antiquities,* book 20, chapter 9.
14. Barclay, page 171.
15. Marshall, page 384.
16. Marshall, page 385.
17. Kent, page 180.
18. Marshall, page 387.

LESSON NINETEEN

# ACTS 27:1-28:31

## Journey to Rome

The story of Acts does not end with the death of Paul, for he is not the only witness Jesus sent "to the ends of the earth" (1:8). But for Luke, who accompanied Paul on his voyage to face Caesar's court, Paul typifies the ambassador of Jesus representing his Lord in every circumstance. Paul has faced a king, governors, scornful philosophers, and lynch mobs; the next stage of his journey holds no more terror for him than those.

As you read 27:1-28:31, imagine how you would have felt and acted on board ship, on Malta, and in Rome with Paul.

### Storm at Sea (27:1-28:16)

***Adramyttium*** (27:2). A port on the coast of Asia, near Troas. The ship was on its way back from Caesarea to its home port. When it reached southern Asia Minor, Julius hoped to find a ship sailing to Rome.

Ancient ships had no rudder and only one sail. They were steered rather clumsily with two large oars (the "rudders" in 27:40), one on either side of the stern (back). Also, they had no compass or sexton, so the sailors needed to see the sun or the stars in order to judge their position and navigate. Finally, there was no way of preserving food for long voyages without restocking. For all these reasons, it was safer to sail from port to port along the coast than directly across the Mediterranean Sea, far from food supplies or a haven from a sudden storm.[1]

***Aristarchus . . . us*** (27:2). Aristarchus may have been heading home to Macedonia, but Colossians 4:10 and Philemon 24 describe him as Paul's companion and fellow prisoner. William Ramsay explained the advantage to Paul of hav ing Luke and Aristarchus along: in the eyes of the centurion and other passengers, these were two of Paul's slaves—his personal physician and his servant. In that status conscious society, Paul thereby acquired the respect due a gentleman; a man without servants was a peon.[2]

***Sidon*** (27:3). Seventy miles (one day's sailing) up the coast from Caesarea. A ship often docked for hours to unload and load goods, so passengers went ashore. The centurion was remarkably generous to let a prisoner off the ship, even though Paul was a Roman citizen not yet convicted of any crime.[3]

***The lee of Cyprus*** (27:4). The direct route would have been to the west and south of Cyprus. However, the prevailing winds in summer were west or northwest, and a ship with one sail could not tack into the wind. So, the ship sailed to the east and north of Cyprus to let the island shield the wind, "keeping close to the coast and taking advantage of the night breeze from off the shore."[4]

***An Alexandrian ship*** (27:6). Egypt produced most of the wheat that fed Italy. Grain ships left Alexandria, sailed straight north to ***Myra*** (27:5), then made their way west. (The northwest winds made it impossible to sail directly from Alexandria to Italy.)[5]

***Cnidus . . . to the lee of Crete*** (27:7). The captain probably wanted to head straight west between Greece and Crete. However, that northwest wind kept forcing the ship to change course and lose time. Cape ***Salmone*** was on the eastern tip of Crete.[6]

***Fair Havens*** (27:8). It was "an open bay, a poor harbour in bad weather."[7] Thus, it was fine as a temporary shelter, but unpromising as a place to spend all winter.

***The Fast*** (27:9). The Day of Atonement, when Jews fasted for repentance. Its date was set by the Jewish lunar calendar, so it varied between September and October. In 59 AD it was on October 5. Because of frequent winter storms in the Mediterranean, shipping was considered hazardous after September 15 and impossible from November 11 to March 10.[8]

***Paul warned them*** (27:9). Apparently, Paul was admitted to a meeting of the sailors and officers, although the centurion overruled his advice.

***Syrtis*** (27:17). These banks of quicksand and submerged rock off the coast of Libya were legendary for sinking ships. They were still 380 miles away, but a storm could drive a ship that far.[9]

***Throw the cargo overboard*** (27:18). To lighten the ship and keep it from sinking; it was probably heavy from filling with water.

***Ship's tackle*** (27:19). Spare gear, such as the mainsail, yardarm, and spars.

***Neither sun nor stars*** (27:20). Without these, the sailors had no idea where they were.

***Adriatic Sea*** (27:27). In ancient times, this included the sea between Italy, Malta, Crete, and Greece.[10]

***Took soundings*** (27:28). "Measured the depth of the sea by letting down a weighted line."[11]

***Dropped four anchors*** (27:29). "To keep the ship's head from swinging round and to prepare the ship to be run ashore when it was light and a suitable opportunity and place could be found."[12]

***276 of us on board*** (27:37). These grain ships were as much as 140 feet long, 36 feet wide, and 33 feet draught (depth in the water).[13] Josephus mentions a ship with 600 people aboard.[14]

**For Thought and Discussion:** a. What do you think of the Maltese view of Justice? Does God always give retribution like this? Why or why not?

b. Does Luke imply in 28:3-6 that there is something superhuman about Paul? Why or why not?

**For Thought and Discussion:** In your opinion, why did Luke describe the ship voyage to Rome at such length—longer than Paul's time in Corinth or Ephesus? What was so important about this episode?

***Kill the prisoners*** (27:42). If the prisoners escaped into the countryside after swimming ashore, the Roman authorities might execute the guards in exchange.

***Islanders*** (28:2). The Maltese were descended from the Phoenicians, who colonized the island centuries earlier. They spoke a dialect of Phoenician rather than Greek, but they were like Roman peasants in culture.[15]

***Justice*** (28:4). To Greeks (and other peoples), Justice was a goddess who assured retribution to the wicked.[16]

***After three months*** (28:11). If they landed in early November, it was now early March. Providentially, another grain ship had been forced to winter in Malta.

***Twin gods*** (28:11). ***Castor*** and ***Pollux*** were the guardian gods of sailors. Their constellation (Gemini) was considered good luck when seen in a storm.[17]

***Syracuse*** (28:12). The leading city of Sicily.

***Rhegium*** (28:13). A town on the toe of Italy, very near Syracuse.

***Puteoli*** (28:13). The main port for Rome at this time, and especially for wheat shipments. The cosmopolitan town included a community of Jews and one of Christians. It was still seventy-five miles south of Rome.[18]

***Spend a week*** (28:14). Luke doesn't say why the centurion was willing to let his prisoner visit with friends.

***Forum of Appius . . . Three Taverns*** (28:15). Two little towns on the Appian Way, the road from Rome south to Rhegium. The former was forty-three and the latter thirty-three miles from Rome.

***Live by himself*** (28:16). Since Paul was not charged with a political or other serious crime, he was not in a prison. He rented his own house or apartment, bought his own food, and was allowed to receive visitors and write letters. He was probably able to carry on his leatherworking as well, in order to support himself. However, he was under guard, perhaps chained, and could not leave his house.[19]

---

1. Briefly summarize what happened on the voyage to Rome (27:1-28:16).

______________________________

______________________________

______________________________

______________________________

______________________________

2. What did Paul say and do during the trip to Rome?

27:9-10 ______________________________

______________________________

______________________________

27:21-26 ______________________________

______________________________

______________________________

______________________________

27:30-32 ______________________________

______________________________

______________________________

______________________________

27:33-36 ______________________________

______________________________

______________________________

______________________________

**For Thought and Discussion:** a. How could Paul, a prisoner, take it upon himself to advise the ship's captain and the centurion, encourage and exhort the crew and passengers, and so on?

b. How is Paul's role in the storm and wreck an example for us?

**For Thought and Discussion:** What do you think the angel meant by saying that God had graciously given *Paul* the lives of his fellow passengers (27:24)? What does this show that Paul had been doing?

**Optional Application:** How can you imitate Paul's attitude toward danger, stress, and hardship?

28:1-6 ______________________________

______________________________

______________________________

______________________________

28:7-10 ______________________________

______________________________

______________________________

______________________________

3. Think about each of Paul's comments and actions. What do you learn about him (his gifts, character, beliefs, attitudes toward people, view of God, etc.)?

______________________________

______________________________

______________________________

______________________________

______________________________

______________________________

______________________________

______________________________

4. Paul's life was saved several times on this trip: land was sighted; the crew did not abandon the passengers; the centurion kept the soldiers from killing the prisoners; nonswimmers could float ashore even thought the ship ran aground; and the viper was somehow harmless.

   a. What did the Maltese natives conclude from all this (28:4-6)?

   ______________________________

   ______________________________

   ______________________________

b. To what do you think Paul and Luke attributed these "lucky coincidences"?

5. Should we conclude from these events that God will always protect His servants—if not from hardship, then at least from death? If so, why? If not, why not, and what should we conclude?

**For Thought and Discussion:** Why do you think Luke wrote so little about the church in Rome? How did his choice of information in 28:17-31 serve his overall plan for Acts?

**For Thought and Discussion:** Why do you think Luke ended Acts where he did? What does this tell you about the theme of Acts?

## Paul preaches in Rome (28:17-31)

Luke knew that Paul was not the first missionary to reach Rome (18:2, 28:14-15). However, he wrote almost nothing about other missionaries or Paul's relations with them, for he was trying to make a particular point in Acts by what he included and excluded.

---

***Jew*** (28:17). The decree of Claudius in 49 AD had been allowed to lapse after his death in 54 AD, so the Jews were now back in Rome.

***We have not received any letters from Judea*** (28:21). Paul's may have been one of the first ships to reach Rome since winter. However, it may also be that the Sanhedrin did not write to Rome. They had little chance of winning their case there (the emperor would not care about a Jewish squabble), and accusers who lost their cases were often punished for filing frivolous suits. Finally, the Jews had only recently been able to return to Rome, so they were not eager to stir up trouble.[20]

**For Thought and Discussion:** a. Why was it so important to Luke to show how Paul related to the Jews?

b. Does Paul's treatment of the Jews have any relevance to us? If so, how? If not, why not?

***We want to hear what your views are*** (28:22). The Jews knew the dispute about Jesus (there were Christians in Rome), and they had probably heard of Paul. They wanted to hear him present his case for Jesus and explain why the leaders in Jerusalem were so mad at him.

---

6. Why did Paul address the Jews when he got to Rome? (*Optional:* See Acts 14:46; Romans 1:16; 9:1-5; 10:1; 11:1-6,11-16.)

7. What did he say to them first (28:17-20)?

8. When they courteously agreed to hear him further, what did Paul go on to discuss with the Jews (28:23)? What specific methods did he use to appeal to them?

9. What was the point of the prophecy from Isaiah that Paul quoted (28:25-29)?

10. How did Paul spend his time awaiting trial (28:30-31)?

11. What good examples does Paul set for all Christians in 28:17-31?

12. What aspect of 27:1-28:31 would you like to apply to your own life?

13. List any questions you have about 27:1-28:31.

**For Thought and Discussion:** In what way were the Jews responsible for their blindness and deafness to the gospel (28:26-27)? Did they want to turn and be healed but God refused, or did they not want this and God gave them their way? (*Optional:* See Romans 9:1-11:32.)

## For the group

**Warm-up.** To help group members compare themselves to Paul, ask, "Have you ever had a life-threatening accident? If so, how did you feel and act?"

**Questions.** Question 5 points out a possible way of misapplying this part of Acts—just because something happens in the narrative, is it necessarily a norm for all time? Romans 8:28-29 may help you draw sound conclusions from Paul's experience.

The quotation of Isaiah in 28:25-29 (question 9) has puzzled many people. Did God arbitrarily make the Jews unable to understand and then hold them responsible? Or, did He decree that they would get what they were asking for?

**Worship.** Praise God for being in total control of every situation, no matter how bleak. Thank Him for the way He acted in Paul's life and for the way He acts in yours.

1. Marshall, page 403; Barclay, pages 183-184.
2. William M. Ramsay, *St. Paul the Traveller and the Roman Citizen* (Grand Rapids, Michigan: Baker Book House, 1949), page 316.
3. Marshall, page 404.
4. Marshall, page 404.
5. Marshall, page 405.
6. Marshall, page 405.
7. Marshall, page 405.
8. Marshall, page 406; Ramsay, *St. Paul the Traveller and the Roman Citizen,* page 322.
9. Marshall, page 409.
10. *The NIV Study Bible,* page 1698.
11. *The NIV Study Bible,* page 1698.
12. Marshall, page 412.
13. Barclay, page 184.
14. Josephus, *The Life,* translated by H. St. James Thackeray, in The Loeb Classical Library (Cambridge: Harvard University Press, 1956), chapter 3.
15. *The NIV Study Bible,* page 1699; Marshall, pages 415-416.
16. Marshall, page 416.
17. Marshall, page 418.
18. Marshall, page 418; *The NIV Study Bible,* page 1700.
19. *The NIV Study Bible,* page 1700.
20. Marshall, page 423; Kent, pages 193-195.

LESSON TWENTY

# REVIEW

Now that you have studied all of Acts, do you remember the themes that run through the book, or are the early chapters already fading from your memory? A review can help you pull together what you've learned so that you can see the book as a whole. The best beginning for a review is to read the whole book again, just as you did in your overview. However, if you prefer, you can skim the book to find answers to the following questions. Your notes on the topics on pages 32-34 and your answers in lesson one will also help you review.

1. From your study of Acts, what would you say the Church is?

_______________________________________

_______________________________________

_______________________________________

_______________________________________

_______________________________________

2. What is the Church's mission?

_______________________________________

_______________________________________

_______________________________________

**For Further Study:** If you've been making an outline, rework it until you are satisfied that it reflects the themes of Acts. If you haven't, make an outline now. The last two books on page 216 may help you learn to outline better.

3. In a few sentences, summarize the Christian message—who Jesus is, what He has done, and how we should respond. (Try to avoid Christian jargon that an unbeliever wouldn't know.)

4. Who is the Holy Spirit?

5. What was His role in the events of Acts?

6. How have you experienced Him acting in your life recently?

7. In Acts, what kinds of things happened to believers when they tried to fulfill their mission and speak their message?

8. Describe some ways in which Peter, Paul, and other believers in Acts responded to opposition and persecution because of the gospel.

9. What is the relationship between Christianity and Judaism, according to Acts?

**Optional Application:** How does the Church's mission apply to you personally? How does it apply to your local church? How are you working on fulfilling your mission?

**For Thought and Discussion:** Make a list of all you have learned about Jesus from studying Acts.

10. What has Acts taught you about Christian fellowship or partnership?

11. In question 7 of lesson one (page 14) you wrote some of the themes of Acts, and you've been tracing them throughout the book. You may also have been working on an outline of Acts from the models on pages 12 and 13. Now, briefly summarize what you think the whole book is about—its main message, purpose, or theme. If you prefer, give the book a title.

12. Have you learned any other important lessons from Acts? If so, explain them here.

13. Have you changed in any ways (thoughts, attitudes, opinions, habits) as a result of studying Acts? If so, how?

______________________________________

______________________________________

______________________________________

______________________________________

______________________________________

______________________________________

______________________________________

14. Look back over the study at questions in which you expressed a desire to make some specific application. Are you satisfied with your follow-through? Or, are there new areas you would like to concentrate on? Pray about plans for further application, and write any notes here.

______________________________________

______________________________________

______________________________________

______________________________________

______________________________________

______________________________________

______________________________________

______________________________________

15. Look at the questions you listed at the end of lessons one through nineteen. Do any remain unanswered? If so, look for answers in some of the sources on pages 213-216, restudy some passage, or talk to a Christian you respect. Record your questions here.

______________________________________

______________________________________

## For the group

**Warm-up.** Say, "Think of one way in which Christian faith affected your actions and attitudes today."

**Questions.** You may have to choose three or four of the themes in questions 1 through 11 to discuss in depth. As you do, ask what difference these truths make to your lives and how your actions can reflect what you have learned from Acts. Then, try together to make up the best possible summary of the book.

Give everyone a chance to answer questions 13 through 15. If possible, let group members answer each others' questions about Acts. Or, direct individuals to cross-references or reference books that give answers. It's always best to help the group do things for itself rather than to have a leader do things for the group.

Some members may feel they have changed little as a result of their study. If so, explore reasons why: How do those members *want* to have changed? Is that want God wants? What has hindered this change? How can your group work on these areas of application together?

**Evaluation.** Take all or part of a meeting to evaluate how well your group has been meeting members' needs and expectations. Here are some questions you might ask:

What did you learn about small group study from your time in Acts together?
How well did the study guide help you grasp the book of Acts?
How did the group discussions help?
What did you like best about your meetings?
What did you like least? What would you change?
How well did you meet the goals you set at your first meeting?
What are members' current needs? What will you do next?

# STUDY AIDS

For further information on the material covered in this study, consider the following sources. If your local bookstore does not have them, ask the bookstore to order them from the publisher, or find them in a seminary library. Many university and public libraries also have these books.

## Commentaries on Acts

Barclay, William. *The Acts of the Apostles* (The Daily Study Bible Series, Westminster Press, 1976).

Instead of verse-by-verse commentary, Barclay gives one page sermons on each passage. His colorful background information and suggestions for application are often helpful.

Kent, Homer A. Jr. *Jerusalem to Rome: Studies in the Book of Acts* (Baker, 1972).

The maps and photographs of this verse-by-verse exposition help make it an excellent resource. Kent is most useful for historical background.

Marshall, I. Howard. *The Acts of the Apostles* (Tyndale New Testament Commentaries, Eerdmans, 1980).

For both theology and verse-by-verse exposition of the text, this is probably the best choice for anyone who does not want to delve into Greek grammar.

## Historical Sources

Bruce, F. F. *New Testament History* (Doubleday, 1979).

A history of Herodian kings, Roman governors, philosophical

schools, Jewish sects, Jesus, the early Jerusalem church, Paul, and early Gentile Christianity. Well documented with footnotes for the serious student, but the notes do not intrude.

Bruce, F. F. *Paul, Apostle of the Heart Set Free* (Eerdmans, 1977).
Possibly the best book around on the historical background and chronology of Paul's life. Bruce explains Paul's personality and thought from an evangelical perspective, although some readers will disagree with his interpretation at points.

Harrison, E. F. *Introduction to the New Testament* (Eerdmans, 1971).
History from Alexander the Great—who made Greek culture dominant in the biblical world—through philosophies, pagan and Jewish religion, Jesus' ministry and teaching (the weakest section), and the spread of Christianity. Very good maps and photographs of the land, art, and architecture of New Testament times.

## Concordances, Dictionaries, and Handbooks

A ***concordance*** lists words of the Bible alphabetically along with each verse in which the word appears. It lets you do your own word studies. An *exhaustive* concordance lists every word used in a given translation, while an *abridged* or *complete* concordance omits either some words, some occurrences of the word, or both.

The two best exhaustive concordances are *Strong's Exhaustive Concordance* and *Young's Analytical Concordance to the Bible*. Both are available based on the King James Version of the Bible and the New American Standard Bible. *Strong's* has an index by which you can find out which Greek or Hebrew word is used in a given English verse. *Young's* breaks up each English word it translates. However, neither concordance requires knowledge of the original language.

Among other good, less expensive concordances, *Cruden's Complete Concordance* is keyed to the King James and Revised Versions, and *The NIV Complete Concordance* is keyed to the New International Version. These include all references to every word included, but they omit "minor" words. They also lack indexes to the original languages.

A ***Bible dictionary*** or ***Bible encyclopedia*** alphabetically lists articles about people, places, doctrines, important words, customs, and geography of the Bible.

*The New Bible Dictionary*, edited by J. D. Douglas, F. F. Bruce, J. I. Packer, N. Hillyer, D. Guthrie, A. R. Millard, and D. J. Wiseman (Tyndale, 1982) is more comprehensive than most dictionaries. Its 1300 pages include quantities of information along with excellent maps, charts, diagrams, and an index for cross-referencing.

*Unger's Bible Dictionary* by Merrill F. Unger (Moody, 1979) is equally good and is available in an inexpensive paperback edition.

*The Zondervan Pictorial Encyclopedia* edited by Merrill C. Tenney (Zondervan, 1975, 1976) is excellent and exhaustive, and is being revised and updated in the 1980s. However, its five 1000-page volumes are a financial investment, so all but very serious students may prefer to use it at a church, public, college, or seminary library.

Unlike a Bible dictionary in the above sense, *Vine's Expository Dictionary of New Testament Words* by W. E. Vine (various publishers) alphabetically lists major words used in the King James Version and defines each New Testament Greek word that the KJV translates with that English word. *Vine's* lists verse references where that Greek word appears, so that you can do your own cross-references and word studies without knowing any Greek.

*Vine's* is a good basic book for beginners, but it is much less complete than other Greek helps for English speakers. More serious students might prefer *The New International Dictionary of New Testament Theology*, edited by Colin Brown (Zondervan) or *The Theological Dictionary of the New Testament* by Gerhard Kittel and Gerhard Friedrich, abridged in one volume by Geoffrey W. Bromiley (Eerdmans).

A ***Bible atlas*** can be a great aid to understanding what is going on in a book of the Bible and how geography affected events. Here are a few good choices:

*The MacMillan Atlas* by Yohanan Aharoni and Michael Avi-Yonah (MacMillan, 1968, 1977) contains 264 maps, 89 photos, and 12 graphics. The many maps of individual events portray battles, movements of people, and changing boundaries in detail.

*The New Bible Atlas* by J. J. Bimson and J. P. Kane (Tyndale, 1985) has 73 maps, 34 photos, and 34 graphics. Its evangelical perspective, concise and helpful text, and excellent research make it a very good choice, but its greatest strength is its outstanding graphics, such as cross-sections of the Dead Sea.

*The Bible Mapbook* by Simon Jenkins (Lion, 1984) is much shorter and less expensive than most other atlases, so it offers a good first taste of the usefulness of maps. It contains 91 simple maps, very little text, and 20 graphics. Some of the graphics are computer-generated and intriguing.

*The Moody Atlas of Bible Lands* by Barry J. Beitzel (Moody, 1984) is scholarly, very evangelical, and full of theological text, indexes, and references. This admirable reference work will be too deep and costly for some, but Beitzel shows vividly how God prepared the land of Israel perfectly for the acts of salvation He was going to accomplish in it.

A ***handbook*** of biblical customs can also be useful. Some good ones are *Today's Handbook of Bible Times and Customs* by William L. Coleman (Bethany, 1984) and the less detailed *Daily Life in Bible Times* (Nelson, 1982).

## For Small Group Leaders

*The Small Group Leader's Handbook* by Steve Barker et al. (InterVarsity, 1982).

Written by an InterVarsity small group with college students primarily in mind. It includes information on small group dynamics and how to lead in light of them, and many ideas for worship, building community, and outreach. It has a good chapter on doing inductive Bible study.

*How to Lead Small Groups* by Neal F. McBride (NavPress, 1990).
Covers leadership skills for all kinds of small groups—Bible study, fellowship, task, and support groups. Filled with step-by-step guidance and practical exercises to help you grasp the critical aspects of small group leadership and dynamics.

*The Small Group Letter*, a special section in *Discipleship Journal* (NavPress).
Unique. Its four pages per issue, six issues per year are packed with practical ideas for small groups. It stays up to date because writers discuss what they are currently doing as small group members and leaders. To subscribe, write to Subscription Services, Post Office Box 54470, Boulder, Colorado 80323-4470.

## Bible Study Methods

Braga, James. *How to Study the Bible* (Multnomah, 1982).
Clear chapters on a variety of approaches to Bible study: synthetic, geographical, cultural, historical, doctrinal, practical, and so on. Designed to help the ordinary person without seminary training to use these approaches.

Fee, Gordon, and Douglas Stuart. *How to Read the Bible For All Its Worth* (Zondervan, 1982).
After explaining in general what interpretation (exegesis) and application (hermeneutics) are, Fee and Stuart offer chapters on interpreting and applying the different kinds of writing in the Bible: Epistles, Gospels, Old Testament Law, Old Testament narrative, the Prophets, Psalms, Wisdom, and Revelation. Fee and Stuart also suggest good commentaries on each biblical book. They write as evangelical scholars who personally recognize Scripture as God's Word for their daily lives.

Jensen, Irving L. *Independent Bible Study* (Moody, 1963), and *Enjoy Your Bible* (Moody, 1962).
The former is a comprehensive introduction to the inductive Bible study method, especially the use of synthetic charts. The latter is a simpler introduction to the subject.

Wald, Oletta. *The Joy of Discovery in Bible Study* (Augsburg, 1975).
Wald focuses on issues such as how to observe all that is in a text, how to ask questions of a text, how to use grammar and passage structure to see the writer's point, and so on. Very helpful on these subjects.